THE DICTIONARY
OF SDI

THE DICTIONARY
OF SDI

BY HARRY WALDMAN

Illustrations by DOUGLAS HOLDAWAY

A Scholarly Resources Imprint
Wilmington, Delaware

The paper used in this publication meets the minimum requirements of the American National Standard for permanence of paper for printed library materials, Z39.48, 1984.

©1988 Scholarly Resources Inc.
All rights reserved
First published 1988
Printed and bound in the United States of America

Scholarly Resources Inc.
104 Greenhill Avenue
Wilmington, Delaware 19805-1897

Library of Congress Cataloging-in-Publication Data

Waldman, Harry.
  The dictionary of SDI.

  1. Strategic Defense Initiative—Dictionaries.
I. Title.
UG743.W35   1987   358'.1754'0321   87-12477
ISBN 0-8420-2281-3
ISBN 0-8420-2295-3 (pbk.)

To Susan, Jonathan, and Laura

Contents

Introduction

"Star Wars"—a phrase that once conjured up the exotic dream world of H. G. Wells, Isaac Asimov, or Stephen Spielberg—is science fiction no longer. Over the last four years, since the media gave the popular tag to President Ronald Reagan's new American space priority, the term has entered into our everyday consciousness. It, or its more technical-sounding alter ego—the strategic defense initiative (SDI)—appears almost daily in news reports: "Iceland Summit Dissolves over SDI"; "Thatcher Supports U.S. Space Initiative"; "American Scientists Oppose Research Efforts in Space-based Missile Defense."

SDI has polarized the scientific community. As spending for SDI-related research continues in America and extends to Europe, critics grow more outspoken as their research status becomes more jeopardized. Meanwhile, issues of practicality, priority, funding, use, and risk divide the community at large. Many of those concerned know little about the system's hypothetical capabilities and proposed methods of deployment, yet studies undertaken to date have not generally helped to clarify the issues. They have tended instead to be either vague, superficial, or imprecise in their terminology, or they have been turgid, jargon-filled, and all but unreadable.

The aim of this dictionary is to clarify and simplify SDI's complex terrain, lay out the technology involved, and identify those areas under debate. The material is presented in a straightforward A-to-Z fashion, with accompanying illustrations in many cases. The emphasis is on terminology, and nearly 800 items are defined in the areas of ballistic missile defense, arms control, research and development, countermoves to defense, Soviet capabilities, the roles of U.S. allies, personalities in the field, and SDI software and hardware. Sources include the SDIO's reports and technical news releases, publications on ballistic missile defense by the Office of Technology Assessment, documents from the Department of Defense and related agencies, and my own experience with ballistic missile systems as a technical analyst on the Sentinel/Safeguard ABM system in the late 1960s and early 1970s.

I have tried to define and explain SDI comprehensively, while stressing such concepts as arms control, defense-dominance, and "transition." The positive has been emphasized because I see SDI as a challenge: SDI might make sense—and justify its cost—if it led to reductions in, or even the elimination of, offensive systems by the United States and the Soviet Union. If it spurred arms control talks and a transition to a defense-dominant strategy by both superpowers, it would be even better.

However, if SDI were to be used by the United States to enhance its offensive posture, this would threaten our strategic balance with the Soviet Union and make a mockery of the Reagan administration's aggressive campaign for public support. Were it to become a program to develop offensive systems in the guise of defense—to seize control of outer space, deploy ASAT weapons, and position them to attack aircraft, power stations, nuclear reactors, dams, and other earth targets—SDI would surely increase the chances for war.

The world is already at the brink of nuclear disaster. Military planners continue to design new weapons to best existing arsenals in an atmosphere of joint distrust. Neither superpower, it seems, trusts itself to do the right thing. The United States presents SDI as its answer to military insecurity, an insurance policy, so to speak, against cheating. It fails, however, to address what SDI means to the Soviet Union, which treats it as another threat, as well it might be, although Moscow also continues to work on its own ballistic defense system. The Soviets would assuredly put up an SDI-like "shield" if they could.

The attempt to achieve mastery over offensive weapons is not new; it goes back to the 1950s and 1960s, from the early Nike-Zeus system, to Sentinel, to Safeguard. But now there is a difference. SDI can open the way to a defense-dominated military position. Even without deployment it could lead to reductions in ICBMs, if SDI is seen as effective. A bilateral, prodefensive strategy spurred by SDI could, theoretically, permit each side a "defensive shield" and, for example, only one-tenth the number of ICBMs. Other nuclear forces could be similarly reduced. Both sides thus would have a guarantee against cheating. However, any belief that SDI could defend us against a full-scale, 10,000-warhead attack is patently absurd and shows the folly of either U.S. military planning or public relations efforts.

This dictionary chooses to emphasize SDI's one kernel of promise: that it may allow us a face-saving way at last to begin to lay down our weapons in security and move away from the specter of nuclear annihilation.

H. W.

THE DICTIONARY
OF SDI

a

ablation: The dissipation of heat generated by atmospheric friction, especially in the reentry of a missile, by means of a heat shield.

ablative: A substance's ability to dissipate the heat of atmospheric friction by means of a melting heat shield. An ICBM booster with an ablative shield or coating could constitute a countermeasure to a directed-energy weapon. *See* countermeasure; hardening.

ablative shock: A theoretical mechanical shock wave that could take place within an object or target exposed to intense, pulsed electromagnetic radiation from a laser or particle beam. As a layer of the object's surface burns off, the resulting vapor would exert further pressure, generating a mechanical shock wave through the rest of the object or target. This shock wave could cause melting, vaporization, spallation (a kind of nuclear reaction), or structural failure of the object.

ABM: Antiballistic missile. *See* BMD.

ABM Treaty: The 1972 treaty, signed and ratified by the United States and the Soviet Union, was designed to slow down the development of offensive systems and limit the bilateral use of ABMs. According to Article VI, each side agrees "not to give missiles, launchers, or radars, other than ABM interceptor missiles, ABM launchers, or ABM radars, capabilities to counter strategic missiles or their elements in flight trajectory, and not to test them in an ABM mode." It restricts both sides to a specified number of land-based units, which could use only rocket interceptors and ground-based radars. The treaty is of unlimited duration. Laboratory research into any type of BMD system is permitted, but there are severe limitations on field testing and development. Only fixed land-based systems can be developed or tested, and only one specified fixed land-based system can be deployed.

　　The Reagan administration has been attempting to justify a "broader" interpretation of the ABM Treaty in order to proceed with the development and possible deployment of SDI. A restrictive interpretation of the agreement, according to some American officials, requires the United States to put off testing of space-based weapons. In effect it limits SDI to the laboratory. The Reagan

3

administration in 1986 proposed a seven-and-one-half-year delay in development of space- and ground-based weapons but would permit testing and development. The Soviet Union in 1985 and early 1986 proposed a fifteen-year moratorium on deployment of new missile defenses. In the Iceland presummit of October 1986, the United States appeared willing to compromise on a ten-year delay, but the Soviet Union wanted to limit SDI to the research laboratory only, prohibiting any testing and development during that ten-year period. This was unacceptable to the United States. Opponents of SDI have formed the National Campaign to Save the ABM Treaty.

Abrahamson, Lt. Gen. James: Director, SDIO, Washington, DC. *See* Strategic Defense Initiative Organization.

absentee ratio: The ratio of the total number of SDI battle stations in orbit to the number in useful defense positions. Not all battle stations could participate at any one time in BMD; some would be wrongly positioned, inoperative, or destroyed. This constantly changing absentee ratio would be a factor in battle-management decisions.

absorption: The process by which atoms and molecules consume energy at certain specific wavelengths. Absorption is a critical phenomenon in the making of lasers and particle beams. *See* emission; laser; particle beam.

accelerator: Also called an atom smasher, the accelerator creates a charged particle beam. All accelerators—whether circular, linear or collective-effect—possess these common features: a source of particles and a means to inject them into the accelerator, a strong electric field to accelerate the particles, a method to handle the beam during acceleration, and a way to extract the beam. The ion accelerator measures in amperes the number of ions emerging every second, and the energy of each accelerated ion in electron volts (eV). The cavities of the latest accelerators make use of superconducting materials, such as niobium, to reduce energy losses of accelerated particles. This, in turn, is stimulating the development of free-electron lasers, which use accelerators. *See* electron volt; free-electron laser; neutral particle beam; particle beam.

accelerator, circular: Also called a cyclotron, a circular accelerator has the advantage of compactness because strong magnetic fields make particles move great distances—as much as 80,000 kilometers over the same circular path.

accelerator, collective-effect: A still theoretical accelerator conceived to achieve high-current and high-energy proton acceleration. It would require large charge densities within an electron beam and strong radial forces to keep protons trapped within waves of the beam.

accelerator, linear: The simplest and oldest kind of accelerator, in which a radioactive material emits charged particles through a long, straight tube. The particles enter the accelerator region at one end and then are accelerated by different methods. The high-speed particles then exit through a hole at the other end of the accelerator. This kind of accelerator offers advantages in the ease of particle injection and extraction but disadvantages in the greater length and size of machinery needed. Its beams tend to spread radially. *See* free-electron laser; neutral particle beam.

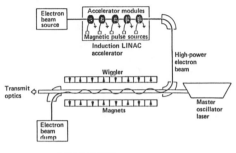

accelerator, linear (induction)

acquire: To detect a target through the use of sensors. The use of neutral particle beam weapons, for instance, would require LWIR sensors for the weapons to be effective.

acquisition: The detection of targets by the sensors of a weapons system. The process of searching for and detecting threatening objects in space. Sensors are designed to search large areas of space and to distinguish potential targets from other objects against the background of space.

acquisition, tracking, and pointing (ATP): A major SDI directed-energy weapons program that will concentrate on laboratory measurements and detection of ICBM booster plumes from space and experiments with the use of passive sensors in the space shuttle bay. The shuttle also may be used in follow-up experiments to explore pointing and tracking technology in any future BMD.

active medium: The collection of atoms that undergoes stimulated emission in lasing. It can be almost anything, including gas, ions, solids, or liquids. *See* lasant.

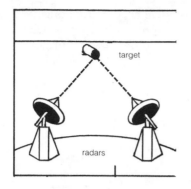 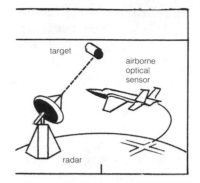

acquisition

active sensor: *See* ladar; sensor, active.

adaptive optics: A method that could be used to compensate for atmospheric distortions to laser beams. As part of the technique called phase conjugation, its use would help undo the bending effects of the earth's magnetic field on ground-based laser (GBL) systems. Successfully demonstrated in an SDI test in Hawaii in late 1985, it calls for a preliminary laser beacon to be sent down through the atmosphere. Any atmospheric distortion would be measured and then reproduced in mirror image in a GBL beam to cancel out any atmospheric effects. Programmed distortions would be made by deformable mirrors, whose shape would be controlled by computers. The computer-controlled mirrors would be able to imprint the obverse of any distorted waveform onto an outgoing beam. *See* ground-based laser; phase conjugation.

advanced test accelerator (ATA): The name of the particle beam accelerator at the Lawrence Livermore National Laboratory.

Airborne Laser Laboratory: An experimental U.S. laser that has been placed on a transport airplane. It has demonstrated the ability of lasers to destroy missiles from various kinds of planes, helped identify fire-control problems, and improved the packaging of lasers to minimize weight and size.

airborne optical adjunct (AOA): A major SDI program that is experimenting with passive airborne optical LWIR sensors to discriminate warheads from decoys. AOA is an aircraft-based, late midcourse- and terminal-phase acquisition, tracking, and pointing system begun in mid-1984. Part of SATKA, the system, which can only do angle tracking and not range-finding, will observe ballistic missile tests

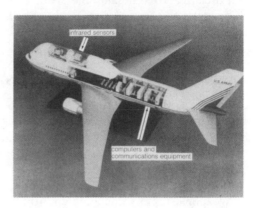

airborne optical adjunct

only at agreed-upon BMD test ranges. The U.S. Department of Defense claims the program is an "adjunct" that will not make use of antimissile components, and thus it will not violate Article V(1) of the 1972 ABM Treaty. A $524-million contract was awarded in July 1984 to Boeing Aerospace, the prime contractor, for completion by 1990. Hughes Aircraft is making the sensor equipment.

The program originally was to have made use of a modified Boeing 767-200 with an 86-foot cupola (upper deck) containing two experimental heat-detecting telescopes (one designed by Hughes Aircraft, the other by Aeroject Electro Systems). Because of cost overruns by July 1986 of $103 million, the more technologically sophisticated Aeroject sensor was eliminated from the program. The design of the ultimate kind of airborne platform, which may carry a crew of fifteen, has not yet been formulated.

air-breathing: Any weapon that travels through the atmosphere and uses air in its propulsion system. Cruise missiles, for example, are air-breathing; ballistic missiles are not.

Air Force Armament Laboratory: The center for design and fabrication of hypervelocity launchers and guns. The emphasis is on improving the mass and velocity of projectiles and the efficiency of launchers. The laboratory is working on a launcher called the *Mark IV*.

Air Force Space Division: As one of five divisions of the U.S. Air Force Space Command, the Space Division (located in Los Angeles) executes the service's research into SDI, particularly as it relates to boost, postboost, and midcourse defenses. The Space Division is doing research on the space-based kinetic-kill vehicle (SBKKV), the boost surveillance and tracking system (BSTS), the space surveillance and tracking system (SSTS), and the heavy-lift launch vehicle (HLLV).

algorithms: The recurrent computations, rules and procedures for solving problems, which for the battle-management/C3 programs of SDI would include situation and damage assessment, defensive firing strategies, and network management. The algorithms would deal with complex engagement problems, the use of different kinds of weapons, rapidly changing environmental conditions, and the need for answers not supplied by the input data. Some algorithms could wait for data in a well-defined system, but others for SDI components would have only a limited amount of data regarding the overall battle situation. Thus, SDI's algorithms might have to be partitioned geographically, have distributed data bases, and still be required to operate effectively were there a loss of communications among some components. The need for highly efficient algorithms presents a strenuous challenge to SDI designers. *See* software; systems analysis/ battle management.

allies: Under Article IX of the ABM Treaty, the United States and the Soviet Union agree "not to transfer to other States, and not to deploy outside its national territory, ABM systems or their components limited by this Treaty." (Agreed Statement G of the treaty further clarifies the issue.) Thus, the Reagan administration's stated plan to share SDI research with its allies in Western Europe and elsewhere is problematic in terms of treaty compliance. The agreement does not limit cooperative laboratory research efforts, but it does prohibit joint development, testing, production, or deployment of ABM systems or components, including fixed land-based launchers and interceptors. Despite these prohibitions, the United States, in 1984, began defense briefings in allied and friendly countries. These briefings covered Soviet activities in strategic offense, the defense and arms control policy implications of SDI, and the scope and progress of SDI research. American defense representatives visited Denmark, Norway, Spain, the Netherlands, and the Federal Republic of Germany in March 1985; Japan in April; Singapore, Malaysia, Indonesia, and Thailand in May; Turkey, China, South Korea, and Australia in June; and in January 1986 a team visited Finland, Sweden, and Switzerland. At the May 1985 economic summit, Reagan briefed the heads of government of Canada, Italy, England, and later that year he briefed NATO allies. *See* France; Great Britain; Israel; Italy; Japan; West Germany.

Alpha/LODE/LAMP: A three-part, SDI directed-energy program. Alpha is a continuous-wave, HF chemical laser being built by TRW for the Defense Advanced Research Projects Agency (DARPA). It is being designed so that it can be launched as a unit and based in space, with 5 megawatts of power. It has a cylindrical combustion chamber made of aluminum. In 1985 the SDIO fabricated an optical resonator, which demonstrated that a high-quality beam could be obtained from the chemical laser. Alpha is located at TRW's San Juan Capistrano test site in California.

Alpha chemical laser

The large optics demonstration experiment (LODE) and the LODE advanced mirror program (LAMP) are experiments in improving beam control and the mirrors that would be used with any laser system. According to SDIO projections, LAMP may achieve a record reduction in density (kilograms/square meter) over that of NASA's space telescope, with segmented elements that are scalable to great sizes. The LODE/LAMP mirror is to be integrated with Alpha by 1990, but this experimental device will be used solely for ground-based testing against stationary ground targets so as not to violate terms of the ABM Treaty.

American Physical Society: National association of physicists which issued a 420-page study entitled "SDI—Directed-Energy Weapons" (April 1987). The report raises doubts that the SDIO can meet its timetable of developing directed-energy weapons by the year 2000. It stresses that, while technological developments are difficult to forecast, much is still unknown about lasers and particle beam weapons. A great deal of technological and engineering work has to be done before scientists will be able to tell if SDI is feasible. The report, which did not deal with kinetic-energy weapons, was developed by a seventeen-member panel which has clearance to investigate the SDIO's work. Kumar Patel of Bell Laboratories headed the panel; Nicolaas Bloembergen, a Nobel Prize winner in laser research from Harvard, was cochairman.

AMOS: An SDI laser test facility in Maui, Hawaii. In 1985 tests there succeeded in propagating a visible laser beam at low power through the atmosphere. In overcoming atmospheric distortions, the tests enhanced prospects for ground-based lasers (GBL); the pointing accuracy was within the tolerances set for any GBL system.

amplified spontaneous emission: *See* superradiance.

analog processing: Computerized problem solving through the direct manipulation of the measure of a physical quantity; for example, the sizes of different voltage pulses may be compared, added, or subtracted in the course of working out a problem. Accurate and high-speed analog processing is considered essential to SDI data processing and the development of software.

antiballistic missile: *See* BMD.

antimatter beam: A theoretical directed-energy weapon in the BMD arena. It would penetrate a target like an ordinary particle beam, but, when it reached the end of its range, it would annihilate a positive particle, thereby releasing a large amount of harmful energy within the target and, in effect, destroying it. The acceleration of antimatter beams would be achieved in the same manner as particle beams. The theory is not as far-fetched as it sounds, since beams of antimatter already have been produced in laboratory research. However, the production of significant quantities of antimatter remains a formidable problem. Moreover, it is not clear that the kill mechanism of such a weapon would justify its serious consideration.

antisatellite (ASAT) weapon: Any weapon that destroys satellites. There is a great deal of overlap between BMD and ASAT technology, but in theory, at least, even a poor BMD weapon could be an excellent ASAT weapon. The Soviet Union's ASAT system was first successfully tested in 1972. While the Soviets' Galosh ABM system was not designed to be an ASAT system, it may have

ASAT capabilities for satellites in orbits similar to ICBM trajectories. (An RV's trajectory outside the atmosphere— peak altitude of 1,000 kilometers with suborbital velocity—is similar to that of a satellite.) The American miniature homing vehicle ASAT weapon (the F-15/ ALMHV) evolved from a design intended for midcourse BMD. Tech-

antisatellite weapon (Soviet)

nologies being investigated for ASAT purposes also may have BMD applications.

The development of an ASAT weapon with BMD capabilities, or upgrading one to such a level, however, would constitute a violation of Article VI of the ABM Treaty, which prohibits the development of ballistic missile defenses. Thus, ASAT weapon development is fraught with controversy. An ASAT system would contain either nondestructive devices (such as jammers and electro-optical countermeasures), or less benign standoff weapons (such as directed- and kinetic-energy weapons, or an isotropic nuclear warhead), and be space-based on a weapons platform or on the ground.

—ASAT Devices—
directed-energy weapons (DEW)
Ground-based: high-power radio waves; lasers; electro-optical countermeasures.
Space-based: high-power radio waves; lasers; neutral particle beams.

isotropic nuclear warhead (INW)
Ground-based: coorbital interceptor; direct-ascent interceptor.
Space-based: space mines.

kinetic-energy weapon (KEW)
Ground-based: coorbital interceptor; direct-ascent interceptor.
Space-based: noncoorbital interceptor.

antisimulation: A countermeasure involving the fooling of an adversary's sensors by making a strategic target appear to be a decoy. In one such deception a balloon would be placed around an RV, thereby disguising the warhead.

antitactical ballistic missiles (ATBM): Defenses against short-range systems used on the battlefield. Since the ABM Treaty speaks only of strategic missiles, ATBM development is permitted. (These missiles were not made part of the treaty because the United States wanted to protect its SAM-D, a surface-to-air missile.) Missiles deployed under the guise of ATBM could limit the effectiveness of shorter range systems and SLBMs and could become so capable that they could defend against ICBMs. In April and July 1986, respectively, the Aerospatiale Company of Paris, the nationalized aerospace firm, and the Konrad Adenauer Foundation in Bonn, West Germany, proposed the development of ATBM systems against shorter range Soviet systems such as the SS-12, SS-21, SS-22, and SS-23 missiles. The ATBM systems could eventually make use of directed- and kinetic-energy weapons developed for SDI. Initially, however, they might use an improved Patriot SAM in West Germany or the new Aster SAM in France. The United States favors development of ATBM systems, but, for political reasons, it is leaving the decision to the Europeans.

AOA: *See* airborne optical adjunct.

apogee: The maximum altitude of a satellite.

Applied Physics Laboratory (APL), Johns Hopkins University: A major Pentagon site for nuclear weapons research in Columbia, Maryland. This institution is one of only two universities among the DOD's 100 main contractors. The work of researchers at this laboratory, which performed nearly $50 million worth of SDI research in 1986, was instrumental in achieving the success of the significant technical milestones (STM) experiment.

architecture: The broad description of all levels of defense, system components, and allocation of jobs among SDI system components. The building blocks of a strategic defense need to be integrated into a coherent and organized whole if they are to be useful and effective. SDI architecture specifies details of system design, including identification, location, and interaction of components. Costs and scheduling influence the architecture, as do the operational constraints of those who will manage, maintain, and deploy it.

Some elements have yet to be clarified (whether system objectives will focus on defending people or missile silos; what is an acceptable range of effectiveness; and what system components can be built under cost constraints), but any archi-

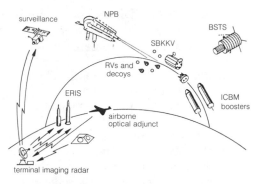

architecture: ground- and space-based weapons (boost and midcourse defense)

tecture still has to concern itself with three key features: 1) constellation size, 2) system survivability, and 3) battle management. The first is a measure of how big the defensive system will have to be to answer the expected threat; the second requires that the defensive system be able to survive an attack upon it; and the third deals with the ability of the components to interact with other parts of the system in order to accomplish their objectives. The most robust architecture would use

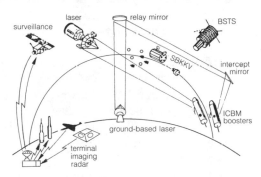

architecture: ground- and space-based lasers

nonnuclear ground- and space-based weapons, along with a neutral particle beam for boost and midcourse defense; another possible architecture is a refinement that would make use of space- and ground-based lasers. A third possibility is a late midcourse and terminal defense that uses KEWs.

One kind of architecture has been proposed by advocates of SDI for early deployment. It also could be designed to defend allies in Europe against shorter range threats. This architecture, a theater defense against tactical ballistic missiles and cruise missiles, would use endo- and exoatmospheric interceptors. Conventional technology—KEW and surveillance satellites—could help to define initial defensive architecture options, while the new technology associated with DEWs could help meet the threats posed by fast-burn boosters. *See* deployment; European defenses; horserace acquisition studies; layered defense; midcourse phase; terminal phase.

area defense: Ballistic missile defense covering large territories. It implies the capability to protect "soft" targets—that is, targets unprotected by either hardened silos or bunkers.

arms control policy: Instead of the pre-1984 approach of seeking reductions in offensive forces, along with the maintenance of the ABM Treaty, U.S. arms control experts in the SDI era have sought greatly reduced levels of nuclear arms and an enhanced ability to deter war by means of conventional defenses against offensive nuclear weapons. The arms control challenge under SDI would be to attain bilateral reductions in offensive weapons while still formulating defenses on both sides. Such a transition agreement would have to be negotiated before actual SDI deployments began, and it might have to take effect during the research and development stages in order to regulate offensive and defensive developments.

The likelihood of negotiating any such agreement that would necessitate measuring, comparing, and monitoring disparate forces is very much in question, particularly after the Soviet rejection of SDI in October 1986. Nevertheless, proponents and opponents of SDI agree that the United States should adopt whatever BMD posture will be most likely to minimize the risk of nuclear war, and that it should carry out some research on BMD technology. In addition, there are grounds for believing that defensive technologies might improve so much faster than offensive technologies that it will become cheaper to deploy defenses than to deploy offensive countermeasures. Proponents say this would give the Soviets a powerful incentive to agree to reduce nuclear arms and concentrate on building their own defensive systems. President Reagan has suggested the possibility of sharing BMD technologies with the Soviet Union. Furthermore, arms control is not simply a matter of opposing the latest lethal devices; instead, it means stabilizing deterrence in order to prevent war. SDI's DEWs, KEWs, and other elements might render the other side's ICBMs and air-breathing vehicles problematic; it also could contribute to prewar deterrence and damage control.

In October 1986 in Iceland, the United States and the Soviet Union appeared tantalizingly close to an agreement on reducing the number of medium-range missiles in Europe, on approving a phase-out of nuclear tests, and on limiting numbers of launchers, missiles, and warheads. What they were unable to agree on was the role of SDI. The Soviets clearly fear SDI and its accompanying new technology, which might put them at a military disadvantage. Without nuclear parity, the Soviet Union is little more than barren. Convincing the USSR to agree to a transition to defensive systems will be a major task. *See* transition.

arms race stability: A strategic balance of forces in which there are reduced incentives for the United States and the USSR to update or expand their respective arsenals to compensate for developments by the other side. Arms race stability is the goal of some SDI theorists who argue that new defensive capabilities might derail arms build-ups. Competition with the Soviets in the development of defensive strategic systems might not be a bad idea, according to some observers, if mutual deployments did not lead to buildups of offensive systems. A defensive race eventually might be self-stabilizing because, if each side could reach a high degree of protection, the competition might then wind down. On the other hand, if SDI developments lead to an escalation of the current arms race, the result would prove costly and monumentally dangerous.

At the very least, both sides could spend billions and feel less secure. This is also a risk. Thus, if the United States goes ahead with SDI, which the Soviets view as a threat to nuclear parity, the range of Soviet responses might include negotiated transitions to defense-dominated strategies and a stable arms control (and reduction) process, unilateral decisions leading to defense-dominated strategies, maintenance of offense-dominated capabilities by employing passive and active countermeasures and increasing the net offensive capability, or both a BMD deployment and additions to offensive capabilities, which would increase instability.

ASAT: *See* antisatellite (weapon).

assured survival strategy: The ability to survive a first strike with minimal losses in life and property. This is the aim of SDI technology. If the United States can "absorb" a first strike and still inflict great damage on the enemy, then it has a retaliation-only strategy. Currently, U.S. nuclear strategy is referred to as countervailing, or mutual assured destruction.

ATA: *See* advanced test accelerator.

ATBM: *See* antitactical ballistic missile.

atmosphere: The gaseous envelope that surrounds the earth and is retained by the earth's gravitational field. One-half of this planet's atmosphere lies below an altitude of 3 miles. At 9 miles there is not sufficient oxygen to sustain life. At an altitude of 28 miles, space begins; it is here that rockets must be used. At 62 miles (100 kilometers) above the earth, the forces that act on ballistic missiles— lift and drag—disappear. At 100 miles above the earth, there is darkness and utter silence. *See* ballistic missile.

atmospheric filtering: The perfect discrimination by a BMD between lightweight decoys and RVs. The system leaves decoys alone and allows them to reenter the atmosphere. The decoys burn up but the heavily shielded RVs do not.

atmospheric heave: A theoretical countermeasure against a neutral particle beam weapon in a boost-phase intercept BMD. The offense extends the protection of the upper atmosphere against any neutral particle beams by exploding nuclear weapons at moderate altitudes before the beams can reach the ascending boosters. The detonations would heat the air, causing it to rise, and effectively raising the altitude at which particle beams would be stripped of their electrons and bent in the geometric field. The neutral particle beam weapon would become ineffective, but the boosters would continue on their trajectories.

atom smasher: A particle accelerator.

ATP: *See* acquisition, tracking, and pointing.

Aurora: A laser system at Los Alamos National Laboratory in New Mexico whose unique feature is its array of computer-controlled mirrors. This permits experimentation with using large relay mirrors to direct laser beams toward their targets. *See* laser; mirrors.

axial: A booster.

B-1 bomber: Built and made operational in 1986, the B-1 is the first long-range strategic bomber developed by the United States in thirty years. It is a supersonic, swing-wing, four-engine jet aircraft. One hundred B-1s and 132 stealth bombers are slated to replace the aging B-52s.

Backus, John: The developer of the Fortran computer language used in scientific applications. Backus believes it is unlikely that fully realizable software can be developed for SDI.

bait-and-switch: An unethical merchandising tactic in which, SDI critics charge, the Department of Defense has engaged. Critics argue that SDI was first proposed to defend U.S. cities and their civilian population, but it is now intended to defend missile silos.

ballistic missile (BM): A missile that is powered by a booster rocket only during its ascent and is in free-fall thereafter. During the initial portion of flight—the boost phase—the missile is most vulnerable. It moves relatively slowly even as it accelerates, its functions depend on rocket motors and guidance systems, it is laden down with tons of explosive fuel, it is easily tracked as it emits a bright infrared plume, and its MIRVs and decoys are still all in the bus. This boost phase, which lasts about 300 seconds, could be shortened with existing technology to perhaps 50 to 90 seconds. The immediately following postboost phase, which takes several minutes, likewise could be made as short as 60 seconds.

ballistic missile

The guidance and control systems of a ballistic missile work as follows: Before launch, projected data for missile position and velocity are fed into the computer; at liftoff, the booster rocket propels the missile into the atmosphere. Guidance applies inertial sensing to measure and record changes in the missile's motion. The resultant calculations then determine the direction in which to steer the rocket so that it will free-fall or coast to its target at the correct velocity. The rocket's control system responds to guidance commands with changes in thrust. When the correct conditions of velocity and position are reached, the guidance system completes the rocket's propulsion and releases the postboost vehicle. The RVs are released and coast in an ellipse until entering the atmosphere, which may slow them down before they explode. Almost the entire cost of a ballistic missile is for the booster and its silo.

Phase	Navigation	Guidance	Control
Boost	Computes position, velocity, altitude	Uses precomputed data, computes velocity corrections	Maintains altitude, directs thrust to meet velocity commanded by guidance
Postboost and midcourse	—	Releases missile at proper altitude and velocity	Changes altitude via thrusters and torques, maintains stabilization, thrusts to new heights
Terminal	—	—	—

ballistic missile defense (BMD) system: Any defensive system that is designed to protect population centers or territory from attacking ballistic missiles. The BMD systems described by the ABM Treaty of 1972 and pursued until 1980 by the United States (and the USSR) consisted of ground-based interceptors of various ranges, supported by ground-based radars. These systems were designed to intercept ballistic RVs as they descended toward the United States, either before or just after they reentered the earth's atmosphere. (The history of American defense systems designed to counteract Soviet ballistic missiles goes back to the late 1950s when the first Soviet ICBMs were introduced. The U.S. defense relied on the Nike missile and a less successful project dubbed BAMBI (ballistic missile boost intercept) involving early KEW projectiles. In the following years the Pentagon pursued similar projects code-named Dynasoar (dynamic soaring), a shuttle-type vehicle that was supposed to shoot anti-missile weapons; Saint (satellite inspection), a sensor designed to detect nuclear weapons in space; Sentinel, the ABM system that relied on nuclear interceptors to protect population centers; and Safeguard, a redrawing of the same Sentinel system but to protect the Minuteman silos instead.

Current BMD concepts posit systems that intercept ballistic missiles and RVs at all stages of flight, from shortly after takeoff to just before detonation. Moreover, BMD is only part of the larger subject of strategic defense, comprising defense against bombers and cruise missiles, civil defense, passive defense of military targets, antisubmarine warfare, and preemptive counterforce attack. Depending on its design, a BMD can operate in one of several modes of defense called completely preferential, semipreferential, or random subtractive.

BMD System: Protection of United States (OTA, 1985)

U.S. Defense	Soviet Offense
5 warning satellites	1,400 ICBMs
160 HF chemical lasers	10 RVs per ICBM
160 ladars	9 midcourse decoys per RV
900 X-ray lasers	1 reentry decoy per RV
900 MWIR trackers	
28,000 midcourse intercept vehicles and boosters	
20 LWIR satellites	
75 radars	
140,000 terminal-phase nonnuclear interceptors	
25 aircraft with LWIR sensors	

battle management: The allocation of resources—sensors and interceptors—within an SDI system under actual or simulated attack; the computer software that would optimize the use of defense resources and the corresponding hardware controlling the operations of a BMD system. Updated battle results would be presented to those in command for analysis and possible reallocation. The efficient appropriation of resources would be critical in a BMD system consisting of many sensors and weapons, each with a limited amount of power or fuel. The need for engagements in space would have to be weighed against weapon capabilities and the apparent enemy strategy. Defensive components also would have to operate within the limited time available. There are five major tasks called for within SDI's battle-management project: algorithms, communications, network concepts, software, and processors. *See* systems analysis/battle management.

battle mirrors: *See* mirrors, intercept.

battle satellite: A satellite—also called a station—in an SDI system that might house as many as fifty lasers or interceptor missiles for boost-phase intercept. Each satellite could weigh 2,500 kilograms and cost $2 billion. In orbit, any battle satellite would spend only a fraction of its time within range of the missile fields where boost phase could occur. This means that, depending on the lethal range of the particular weapons SDI employed, there would have to be ten to thirty satellites in orbit for every one within range of its targets. This problem does not negate the technical feasibility of such a defense, but it does present a serious economic obstacle to implementation. The offense can drive up the number of battle stations required—and thus the cost of a defensive system—by simply increasing the number of ground boosters that would have to be intercepted. Similarly, it could drive up costs by hardening the boosters, decreasing the lethal range of each defensive weapon, and using fast-burn boosters. These problems seem to prohibit predeployment of unmanned battle satellites until means are found to make them cheaper to build and deploy, and harder to detect and destroy in space. (However, they would not rule out early-warning satellites, which would be necessary for any defense.) *See* constellation size.

beam director: The beam control system that receives a laser beam and prepares it for passage either through the atmosphere or through space. For a laser beam the atmosphere changes 1,000 times per second. Therefore, a beam passing through the atmosphere will have to be adjusted frequently. SDI researchers are working to improve state-of-the-art technology to allow phase conjugation and adaptive optics to overcome atmospheric interference. A low-energy laser beacon would have to be fired from a relay mirror down to a ground-based system to tell it how the atmosphere is changing. The beacon will have to produce a certain number of pulses per second to be useful. At the same time, a cooled deformable mirror with actuators would be needed by the beam director to beam its laser up. *See* ground-based free-electron laser.

Bear F: A Soviet strategic bomber that can carry ten cruise missiles.

Bethe, Hans: Nobel Prize physicist, now at Cornell University, who opposes SDI, believing it futile and dangerous. He argues that SDI would be vulnerable to preemptive attack, to "underflying" by SLBMs and other craft, and to overwhelming waves of attacks and the use of decoys. Moreover, Bethe maintains, SDI would cost too much and would destabilize arms control. He is coauthor of *The Fallacy of Star Wars* (1984).

birth-to-death tracking: The tracking of all threatening objects from the instant they are deployed by a booster or postboost vehicle until they are detonated, or "killed." *See* SATKA.

Blackjack: A Soviet strategic bomber that can carry ten cruise missiles.

blackout: The disabling of a radar system by a nuclear explosion. The intense electromagnetic energy released in the explosion generates a large background, which obscures signals and creates interference of radar, thereby rendering it useless.

"black program": The SDIO's highly classified program for developing a blueprint for deploying strategic defenses by 1994. This is proceeding either without formal public presidential consent or with secret presidential consent. Based on a careful review of a reorganization that is under way within the SDI program, the tasks assigned to defense contractors, and SDIO's internal transfer of fiscal year 1987 funds and the proposed 1988 budget from the more exotic directed-energy weapons programs to kinetic-energy systems, congressional sources believe that the Pentagon has made the decision to deploy SDI in the near-term. These sources believe the architecture would only have an effectiveness of 16 percent against Soviet missile warheads. Such a deployment in 1994–95 would have no laser or beam weapons, no midcourse kill or discrimination capabilities to speak of, a token deployment of space-based kinetic-kill vehicles (SPKKV) for defense in the boost phase that would likely be able to destroy no more than 11 percent of the Soviet offensive threat, and 400 to 1,000 ground-based terminal-phase interceptors (ERIS and HEDI) that might destroy no more than 5 percent of the incoming warheads. A near-term deployment of SBKKVs would have a military utility in space of perhaps five to ten years as the Soviets respond with countermeasures.

Access to this SDI architecture is compartmentalized so that only a few members of Congress have reviewed it or know of its existence. The architecture is said to be the one proposed by the George C. Marshall Institute in late 1986. SDI scientists themselves are concerned that long-term research will be sacrificed to pay for the huge cost of near-term deployment, particularly in the area of kinetic-energy weapons and space transportation. There is also the serious question of what the United States does after near-term deployment of SDI. *See* deployment.

bleaching: The phenomenon in which X-rays from a nuclear explosion conceivably destroy enough electrons in the atmosphere so that the X-rays themselves pass unaffected through the air. This physical effect could permit a highly concentrated and bright X-ray laser in space to penetrate the atmosphere—perhaps by 16 kilometers or more—and be used against fast-burning boosters, hitting any targets 120 kilometers above the earth. By the same token, this phenomenon could allow an X-ray laser, located within the atmosphere, to become an offensive weapon, bleaching its way through the air against targets in space. *See* X-ray laser.

Blechman, Barry M.: Coauthor with Victor Utgoff of the paper "Fiscal and Economic Implications of Strategic Defense" (1986). The authors prepared the study (since published in book form) for the Johns Hopkins Foreign Policy Institute, which was investigating the military uses of space. They posited four national strategic defense systems and their costs. The simplest system, identified as alpha, is basically a terminal defense composed of long- and short-range interceptors, early-warning aircraft, and long- and short-range surveillance aircraft with interceptor missiles. The second, or beta, system adds interceptors to safeguard nearly fifty major cities. Gamma, the third type of defense, adds a boost-phase layer of low-orbit satellites with interceptor missiles (KEWs) controlled by battle stations at 5,000 kilometers. Finally, delta, the most complex system, is a multilayered BMD composed of chemical lasers for boost-phase interception in the beta defense. The first two systems, the authors claim, could be operational by the year 2005, the third by 2012, and the fourth by 2020. Projected costs range from $170 billion for the beta defense, to $670 billion for delta, to $770 billion for gamma.

Alpha:
> Would protect U.S. retaliatory forces.
> BMD systems: ground-based interceptors, long-range surveillance aircraft with air-to-air missiles, early-warning aircraft, short-range interceptors.
> Ten-year cost: $160 billion.
> Fully operational: 2005.

Beta:
> Would protect U.S. retaliatory forces and fifty major cities.
> BMD system: alpha plus interceptors to protect population centers.
> Ten-year cost: $170 billion.
> Fully operational: 2005.

Gamma
> Full defense against Soviet ICBMs, IRBMs, and aircraft.
> BMD system: same as beta plus battle-management satellites in high orbit, missile interceptors in low orbit.
> Ten-year cost: $770 billion.
> Fully operational: 2012.

Delta
> SDI-type system that would defend against Soviet ICBMs, IRBMs, and aircraft.
> BMD system: same as beta plus satellites in high orbits, chemical lasers in low orbits.
> Ten-year cost: $670 billion.
> Fully operational: 2020.

BM: battle management.

BM/C3: BM/command, control, and communications.

BMD: ballistic missile defense. The most common of four roughly equivalent acronyms that identify defense against nuclear ballistic missiles. Such defenses used to be called antiballistic missile (ABM) systems, but the designation fell out of favor after the demise of the Sentinel and Safeguard systems by the early 1970s. Since then the acronym BMD has replaced ABM as the term of choice. Within the last few years the more clearly defined defense against ballistic missiles (DABM) has gained some popularity. The BMD efforts signifying President Ronald Reagan's "Star Wars" program are referred to as SDI. Normally the phrase "strategic defense" encompasses other methods of limiting damage from nuclear attack besides BMD.

BMD components and systems: The major elements within any SDI architecture. A highly capable system would meet the following "challenging" requirements:

- a boost-phase defensive layer effective in the face of proliferation and countermeasures, including rockets with boosters that finish burning very quickly and upper stages that rapidly dispense their separate RVs;

- sensors and computers that discriminate between decoys and RVs in the midcourse phase, as objects separate from the postboost vehicles but before they reenter the atmosphere;

- sensors that function nearly continuously under attack and against a background of nuclear detonations;

- a system of battle-management computers and software of extremely high complexity;

- a control system that will track targets, assign weapons to targets, account for targets destroyed, and assign other weapons to missed targets;

- communications that link sensors, battle-management centers, and weapons that function despite jamming attempts, attacks, and interference from nuclear detonations;

- space-based power supply stations, each providing 10 megawatts or more;

- the means to protect space-based BMD assets from attack; and

- numerous ground-based exoatmospheric interceptors for the late midcourse layer and endoatmospheric interceptors for the terminal layer.

booster: That stage of a rocket that provides thrust after launch. It "boosts" the payload, accelerating it from the earth's surface into a ballistic trajectory, during which no additional force is applied to the payload. The boost profile of the U.S. MX missile is as follows: Pressure from a steam generator expels the missile from its storage cannister, or silo. Once clear of the cannister, the missile ignites the first-stage motor, which burns for about 55 seconds, up to an altitude of 22 kilometers. The second stage also burns for 55 seconds, taking the rocket to 82 kilometers. The last stage of the

booster

booster will burn for 60 seconds and take the rocket to 200 kilometers, the altitude of the lowest orbiting satellites. The last few seconds of the third-stage burn are crucial for giving the payload enough speed to reach its target, because any disruption up to burn-out will cause the warheads to fall far short of their targets. The Soviet ICBM arsenal today comprises about 1,400 boosters, more than two-thirds of them MIRVed; most are slow-burning, liquid-fueled. The U.S. arsenal contains 1,000 fast-burning, solid-fueled Minuteman boosters, about one-half of them MIRVed. Both sides have been adding solid boosters to their arsenals since 1980.

ICBM	Type	Wt(kg)	Length (m)/ Width (m)	Burnout (secs)/ Altitude (km)
SS-18 (10 RVs)	2-stage liquid	220,000	35/3	300/400
MX (10 RVs)	3-stage solid	89,000	21/2	180/200 (busing ends at 650 secs/ 1,100 km)
Fast-burn MIRVs	2-stage solid	87,000	23/2	50/90 (busing ends at 60 secs/110 km)
Midgetman (1 RV)	2-stage solid	19,000	12/2	220/340
Low-flight Midgetman	2-stage: 1 solid, 1 liquid	25,000	13/2	220/100
Fast-burn Midgetman	2-stage solid	20,000	14/2	50/80
Hardened Midgetman (1 gm/cm squared shielding)	2-stage: 1 solid, 1 liquid	30,000	15/2	220/320
Pershing II	2-stage solid	7,500	11/1	100/–

ICBM Booster Features

boost phase: The first phase of a missile's trajectory, during which the first- and second-stage engines are burning. The boost phase lasts from launch to burnout of the final stage. For ICBMs the length of this phase is currently from three to five minutes, but studies show that it can be reduced to less than one minute. During boost phase the rocket produces a "signature" of easily detectable hot exhaust gases as it rises above the clouds and the denser layers of the atmosphere. It is during boost phase that infrared

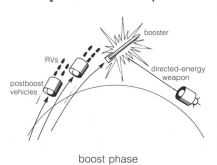

boost phase

sensors, even those based on satellites 32,000 kilometers away, would have to track a missile by its rocket signature.

For defense systems the detection, tracking, and overcoming of enemy boosters are complicated by any compression of the boost phase or the rocket signature, and consequently the time to react. Solid-fuel rockets, for example, are harder to track because they can accomplish fast burn, with a less permanent signature, than liquid-fuel rockets. Future fast-burn boosters, which could conceivably reduce burn time to 40 seconds, would make boost-phase interception even more difficult. Moreover, not all of the boost phase is available for the defense to overcome the boosters. The defense must first detect the launchings, determine if there is an attack, decide whether to engage the boosters, and then allocate defensive weapons, all within the space of a few minutes.

In planning SDI, engineers are allowing for still less reaction time. They project that any decisions to launch interceptor rockets from satellites, fire projectiles from an electromagnetic railgun, or shoot lasers or particle beams would have to be made within 10 seconds of an ICBM launch. Interception then would need to take place within about 20 seconds after the booster rockets shut off and when all the RVs would still be on the bus. Boost-phase BMD schemes are as old as the space age (*see* ballistic missile defense), but DEW technology has introduced new possibilities. Boosters are now vulnerable to high-energy, long-wavelength chemical lasers about 30 seconds after launch. None of the other kinds of lasers, it appears, can reach very far into the atmosphere; they must wait 90 seconds or so after launch to be effective against boosters emerging from the protection of the atmosphere. All but a few of the short-wavelength lasers, particle beams, and X-ray lasers are absorbed by even a thin layer of air and cannot penetrate below about 110 kilometers. SBKKVs would have to fly down into the atmosphere, but they would heat up and their infrared sensors immediately blinded. Future boost-phase interception also could be considered in a defensive architecture against shorter range tactical ballistic missiles that could threaten Europe.

boost surveillance and tracking system (BSTS): The major SDI experimental system (part of SATKA) designed to demonstrate the technology needed to upgrade the current satellite early-warning system. Specifically, BSTS would identify ballistic missile launchings and objects entering space. It would have to be highly survivable itself against any attack and be able to hand over data to other defense elements after the boost phase. The program could conceivably contribute to an early-warning system against attack, but the U.S. Department of Defense states that "it will not be given the capability to process launch detection data in real time." Thus, the BSTS would not violate Article V(1) of the ABM Treaty, which bans the development, testing, and deployment of space-based ABM components. Although

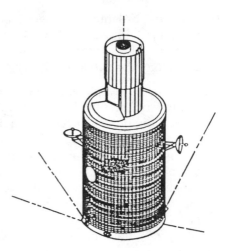

boost surveillance and tracking system

the system would collect ballistic missile plume data under current plans, it would not perform any real-time data processing for the transfer of information to a boost-phase interceptor. The BSTS is the more mature of SDI's space-based sensor technologies.

bremsstrahlung: German for "braking radiation"—that is, the means by which a charged particle emits radiation when it encounters a molecule of air. It loses energy as it accelerates or decelerates. High-energy radiation, particularly *bremsstrahlung*, is sometimes referred to as gamma radiation.

brightness: The measure of the source intensity of a DEW; the amount of a DEW's power and a basic measure of lethality, expressed in megawatts. Brightness is proportional to the size of the cone into which a laser is directed. *See* 10-kilojoule criterion.

Broad, William J.: Science writer for the *New York Times* and author of *Star Warriors* (1985). Broad has written extensively on SDI.

Brooks, Frederick P., Jr.: Developer of the software for the IBM 360 system and professor of computer science at the University of North Carolina. Brooks defends the feasibility of SDI, maintaining that it is possible to develop effective software for the system.

BSTS: *See* boost surveillance and tracking system.

Buchsbaum, Solomon: Vice president of Bell Telephone Laboratories in Murray Hill, New Jersey. Buchsbaum, who serves as an adviser on technical issues to governmental agencies, insists that existing technology can produce adequate SDI software.

bus: The postboost-phase vehicle of a ballistic missile; the remainder of a missile after the last stage is jettisoned. The intercept of a bus poses difficult challenges. It requires a different sensor than does booster tracking since the bus's plume is much less conspicuous, and its rocket motor may not operate continuously. Once the bus jettisons its RVs, it becomes less important. At this point it operates above the atmosphere, where it may deploy lightweight shields, decoys, and other countermeasures to detection. However, once it enters space, it is vulnerable to attack by particle beams, which cannot penetrate the atmosphere. *See* postboost vehicle.

C

C2: *See* command and control.

C3: command, control, and communications.

CADE: *See* combined allied defense experiment.

capital satellite: A highly valued or costly satellite or decoy.

carbon/graphite: The fibers that are the chief reinforcements in advanced composites, exhibiting high strength and high elasticity. A carbon-fiber ballistic missile coating could reflect lasers and pose as a possible countermeasure to a DEW. Some studies have shown that even a few grams of such a coating per square centimeter might enhance the survivability of a booster by twenty to thirty times. *See* countermeasure.

Carnesale, Albert: Dean of the Kennedy School of Government, Harvard University, who has written extensively about nuclear issues. He has said that a leak-proof SDI system would constitute a defense of U.S. society overall and could lead to vast reductions in, or even the elimination of, nuclear weapons. Carnesale also has warned, however, that using SDI to defend only U.S. retaliatory forces would bolster the policy of mutual assured destruction.

Carter, Ashton: Author, former Pentagon analyst, and member of the Kennedy School of Government at Harvard University. A critic of SDI, he wrote "Directed Energy Missile Defense in Space" (1984) and *Ballistic Missile Defense* (1984).

CCCI: command, control, communications, and intelligence.

ceramic: An inorganic, nonmetallic solid. The production of ceramics for military use is expected to grow substantially in the next quarter century. Ceramics is being considered for use in missile bearings, rocket nozzles, laser mirrors, and railgun components. *See* composite.

chaff: A countermeasure to a ballistic missile defense that takes the form of confettilike, metal-foil ribbons that can be ejected from a spacecraft in order to reflect enemy radar signals and electromagnetic energy. The aim is to create false targets, or to screen actual targets from the view of radar. Chaff also can be dropped from shells and rockets.

charged particle beam: *See* particle beam.

CHECMATE: compact high-energy capacitor module advanced technology experiment. *See* Maxwell Laboratories.

chemical laser: Laser radiation produced by the chemical reaction between two fuels. The active medium resembles a rocket engine. The most mature technology (lasant) for a high-powered chemical laser is either hydrogen fluoride (HF, having a wavelength of 2.7 microns), or deuterium fluoride (DF, having a wavelength of 3.8 microns). The chemical laser is viewed as having good potential for space-basing. Its overall efficiency is good, and relatively high levels of power already have been attained, although not yet at levels needed for any SDI system.

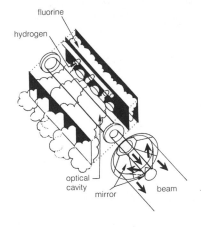

chemical laser

Until most recently the chemical laser for SDI architectures has been the early favorite DEW because of its ability to penetrate the upper atmosphere. The MIRACL and the Alpha laser, both being developed by TRW, are examples of this kind of laser. However, according to projections by the Office of Technology Assessment in 1984 and 1985, large volumes of chemicals would be needed to fend off an attack. The destruction, for instance, of 1,400 enemy boosters would require some 300,000 kilograms of chemicals to be in position over the aggressor's ICBM fields, out of perhaps 10 million kilograms in orbit worldwide. The remaining components of the chemical laser defense system—sensors, aiming and pointing technology, and communications—would be the same as for any DEW system.

To thwart countermeasures making enemy boosters more resistant to attack, lasers would need greatly increased brightness levels. These still hypothetical lasers would have extremely short wavelengths (the current SDI target is 1 micron) and greater power. Relay and battle mirrors might have to be enlarged to achieve this. Other chemical lasers are also under consideration: oxygen-iodine (1.3 micron wavelength), iodine fluoride (0.65 and 0.72 microns), and nitrogen oxide (0.24 microns). The free-electron laser, however, may be able to meet the requirements for an effective DEW. *See* Alpha/LODE/LAMP; deuterium fluoride; free-electron laser; hydrogen fluoride; laser; MIRACL; 10-kilojoule criterion.

Hypothetical SDI Systems with Chemical Lasers
(Adapted from OTA Reports, 1985)

Chemical Laser Battle Stations (20 megawatts)	Enemy Boosters	Hardness (kj/cm sq.)
150	1,400	10
300	2,800	10
500: altered enemy deployment pattern	1,400	10
1,000: increased booster hardness	1,400	60
30: laser brightness increased 100 times (80 megawatts)	1,400	10
1,000: against fast-burn boosters (50 seconds)	1,400	10

---

chemical laser, short-wavelength: *See* chemical laser.

Cobra Judy: A U.S. sea vessel used to observe Soviet ballistic missile tests and to collect data on ballistic missile RVs, missiles, and warheads. A new radar recently has been installed on the ship.

Cobra Judy

coherence: The moving in step of waves of light and beams of radiation. Traverse coherence describes the matching of such rays in space, while temporal coherence describes · their matching in time. When matched, the wave structures of parallel rays travel at a single frequency of electromagnetic

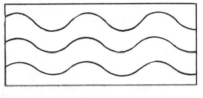

coherence

radiation, thus reinforcing the energy of the components and creating a larger beam. Lasers and radar systems produce coherent radiation, which means that all the waves of radiation maintain a crest-to-crest and trough-to-trough alignment. Coherent waves, or beams, strike a surface with greater effect. Coherent radiation may be visible, infrared, ultraviolet, or X-ray. *See* laser.

cold body: An object that gives off infrared radiation at or near low ambient temperatures. All objects radiate electromagnetic energy. If the object is hot enough, the energy takes the form of visible light.

combined allied defense experiment (CADE): A program within the SDIO's antitactical ballistic missile defense effort that will support the development of the theater defenses for Europe.

command and control: The method of controlling satellites, battle stations, and other SDI components; a function of battle management that integrates the workings of all the separate components and that must be able to run on its own. This function would comprise communications links among components, data processing to support sensors and battle station operations, and battle-management software, including all instructions and decisions for defense and coordination with offensive forces.

command guidance: The steering and control of a missile by the transmission of commands. *See* guidance.

communications: A task within SDI's battle-management project that will examine the design, planning, and the means of transmission of messages within any SDI architecture. *See* battle management.

compliance: Adherence to the provisions and interpretations of the ABM Treaty, as it applies to the United States and the Soviet Union. In evaluating the experiments planned for the SDI program, the Reagan administration has said it will interpret the treaty's provisions based on single-standard assessments of capabilities for each side rather than on subjective judgments as to intent. It is an open question whether SDI research will avoid development, testing, and deployment of ABM components that are sea-based, space-based, air-based, or mobile land-based in order to maintain compliance. However, the SDI program will certainly research new devices short of field testing of a prototype ABM system or component; therefore, any new devices developed will not be subject to stricter standards than existing systems. Finally, since the treaty restricts defenses against only strategic ballistic missiles, SDI is free to deploy defenses against nonstrategic (tactical) ballistic missiles and cruise missiles.

The undersecretary of defense for research and engineering (USDRE) is responsible for ensuring that all defense programs are in compliance with existing strategic arms limitation agreements. No project or program that raises the issue of compliance is supposed to enter into testing, prototype, construction, or deployment phases without prior clearance from the USDRE. There are three types of activities that are permitted by, and judged in compliance with, the ABM Treaty: 1) conceptual design or laboratory testing, which precedes "field testing," is considered to be research, and thus not subject to verification by national technical means (NTM) nor bound by treaty limitations; 2) field testing of devices that are not ABM components or prototypes of ABM components (*see* tested in an ABM mode), and that do not give non-ABM launchers, missiles, or radars the capabilities to attack strategic ballistic missiles; and 3) field testing of fixed land-based ABM components, which is permitted provided it meets with certain criteria, among them that it takes place at agreed-upon ABM test ranges—White Sands Missile Range and Kwajalein Missile Range—and the number of test launchers does not exceed fifteen. *See* ballistic missile defense; Soviet Union.

component: According to the 1972 ABM Treaty, this term is defined as an ABM radar, launcher, or interceptor missile. However, the research and development community uses the term "component" to describe any part, down to the smallest switch, that helps make up an ABM system or subsystem.

composite: Any combination of particles and fibers in a common matrix (the material that binds the reinforcement together and transmits loads between reinforcing fibers). Composites of all types—ceramic, polymer, and metal-matrix—are considered ideal for SDI applications. Their properties of low density, high specific stiffness, low coefficiency of thermal expansion, and high temperature resistance are all necessary for structures that will have to maneuver rapidly in space, maintain high-dimensional stability, and withstand attack. An SDIO program committed to the development of new materials and structures is studying the use of composites in lightweight structures, thermal and electrical materials, optical materials and processes, tribology (the study of the phenomenon and mechanisms of friction, lubrication, and wear of surfaces in relative motion), and materials durability.

concept formulation and technology-development planning: That facet of the DEW program responsible for evaluating the technical requirements of the weapons under consideration.

cone: The geometric shape formed by a laser beam. Cone size is measured in units called steradians. A divergence angle of x radians results in a cone size of $\Pi x^2/4$ steradians.

Consolidated Space Operations Center: The National Test Facility for SDI research at Falcon Air Station in Colorado Springs. *See* national test bed.

constellation size: The number of weapons platforms, such as satellites and rockets, in a potential SDI system needed to perform boost-phase intercept. If the offense increases its number of ICBMs or decreases the burn time for boosters, a defense system must meet an attack more quickly. This might necessitate an increase

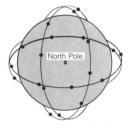

constellation size. A hypothetical arrangement of thirty-two chemical laser battle stations at 1,000-kilometer orbits; range: 4,000 kilometers

in constellation size, depending on the capacity of the BMD to handle the load. Other factors that can influence constellation size are weapon brightness, slew time, constellation altitude, and the size and distribution of the threat. *See* slew time.

continuous-wave laser: A laser whose coherent light is generated continuously rather than at fixed time intervals. Continuous-wave lasers include the free-electron laser and the chemical laser, which would deliver radiant thermal energy to targets. Contact would be maintained until the laser burned a hole through the target, or the temperature of the target reached damaging levels.

control: The application of corrective actions to meet guidance requirements, for instance, for an ICBM; the application of forces to a vehicle to meet stated variables. *See* ballistic missile; guidance.

CONUS: continental United States.

Convention on Registration: The 1974 United Nations agreement requiring all countries to register objects launched into outer space. Information required includes date of launch, territory from which objects were launched, orbital parameters (apogee, perigee, inclination), and functions of objects.

coorbital satellite interceptor: A killer satellite, or antisatellite weapon, believed to have been developed by the Soviet Union in 1972, effective against satellites in altitudes of 5,000 kilometers, depending on orbital inclination. A prototype was launched from the Soviet Union's Tyuratam complex. Under the existing ABM Treaty, coorbital interceptors are permitted, but they must be ground-launched and nonnuclear. They also can be predeployed as nonnuclear space mines.

corner reflector: A countermeasure to laser radars (ladars). Corner reflectors affixed to a target would produce reflected light that would be picked up by laser radars. Likewise, any reflectors put on rockets or ejected from a target might force the beam weapon to attack them instead of the target itself.

cost-effectiveness: The total system cost for SDI will remain difficult to predict for some time. The first six years of the program are scheduled to consume more than $30 billion in defense research funds, but a system that led to negotiations of deep reductions in offensive forces could eventually result in a smaller budget for offensive weapons. The burden of providing cost estimates should fall to those who maintain that an effective SDI system will be affordable, including those whose job it is to define potential system architectures.

SDI Budget Projections ($Billions)	
1984	1.0
1985	1.4
1986	3.7
1987	4.9
1988	6.2
1989	7.3
1990	8.6

cost-exchange ratio: A factor in considering whether SDI is feasible. In theory, the employment of defensive measures should cost less than the continued buildup of offensive ones, or, put another way, any increments in defense should cost less than the corresponding increments in offense they are to meet. If this is so, then the Soviet offense should have a strong disincentive to try to match new defense systems with offensive weapons. This is one goal of an affordable SDI system: to identify a system wherein the cost of overcoming both existing Soviet offenses and presumed countermeasures is affordable. If a battle station were to achieve a 1:30 kill ratio against enemy boosters, for instance, to be effective it should not cost more than thirty times that of a booster. If it did, the offense could force the defense to spend too much to stay ahead. A cost of $50 million per booster would mean that the defense could spend 1.5 billion per battle station and still maintain a favorable cost-exchange ratio. At $200 million per booster the defense would have to keep costs below $6 billion per station.

counter-countermeasures: An action taken to defeat countermeasures. While counters to all possible countermeasures do not exist, ideas have been suggested for some because any SDI system must try to anticipate all possibilities. For example, if the defense develops a method to measure the mass of objects in space, the offense will not be able to rely on decoys to fool sensors. Or, if the defense develops effective postboost and midcourse phase defenses (accurate discrimination and fast weapons), the need for a boost-phase defense layer would be reduced and the threat of fast-burn ICBMs lessened. Finally, if the offense hopes to overwhelm the defensive system by means of a mass, simultaneous launching of ICBMs, a defensive system, programmed to meet just such a threat, would be an effective counter-countermeasure.

counterforce blow: A strike by the offense that substantially weakens the enemy and limits any retaliation to what the offense considers an "acceptable" level. To prevent a counterforce blow, conventional BMD systems have been designed to protect hard targets such as ICBMs. The goal is not necessarily to protect every shelter but to assure the survival of sufficient retaliatory forces to raise the "price" of a successful attack.

countermeasure: An action taken by an attacking system to overcome identification and interception by the defensive missile system. In common usage it means any of a number of specific responses the Soviet Union could take to defeat SDI. A countermeasure may be technical (against hardware), or tactical (to overcome the effectiveness of the BMD). Countermeasures available against sensors and discrimination could include blinding, spoofing, and hiding; countermeasures against weapons could include hardening, using fast-burn boosters, coating missiles with carbon fibers to reflect lasers, and putting a spin on warheads so that lasers and particle beams cannot fix on a single spot. These fall under the general categories of saturation, evasion, and defense suppression.

The offensive usually pays a price for countermeasures, which, although they confuse one part of a defensive system, may increase the offense's vulnerability to another. Thus, while a fast-burn rocket avoids several types of defense weapons, its postboost vehicles and decoys cannot usually deploy within the atmosphere lest nuclear weapons used as suppressing or blinding agents disable the offense's own space assets. Similarly, decoys that imitate RVs require heavy thrusters that would reduce the available throw-weights of ICBMs. Hardened boosters would reduce the available throw-weights for real warheads. Within the SDI program, special groups of analysts are responsible for envisioning Soviet countermeasures. These experts compose what is known as the Soviet red team, the technical red and blue teams, and a team of mediators. The Soviet red team is interested in possible Soviet responses to SDI; the technical red and blue teams will assist defense designers in studying the U.S. Army's high-endoatmospheric interceptor (HEDI) system, now under development. The mediators—a group of senior governmental and industry advisers—will report on the findings of the red and blue teams to the chief scientist within SDIO. *See* defense suppression; laser.

—Countermeasures—

active
Shoot-back, attack, retaliation.

passive
Hiding, deception, evasion, hardening, electronic and electro-optical, proliferation.

countermeasure, electronic: An action designed to overcome sensor discrimination. It might take the form of jamming (overloading enemy receivers with strong signals), or spoofing (sending deceptive signals).

countermeasure, electro-optical: The overcoming of sensor discrimination by means of dazzling (temporary blinding) and spoofing techniques.

countermeasure, passive: A nondestructive action to offense or defense intended to confuse the enemy. An example of a passive countermeasure might be the concealment of radar instruments to reflect signals only weakly, to maintain radio silence, or to signal covertly to prevent detection by military satellites.

countervailing strategy: The current U.S. posture with regard to the use of nuclear weapons. It attempts to deter attack, or the threat of attack, on the United States and its allies by persuading the Soviet Union that U.S. nuclear counterattacks would lead to unacceptable damage to Soviet assets and would cause the USSR to fail in its geopolitical objectives.

counting rules: Rules that aim to simplify the verification of mathematical limits imposed by negotiations.

crisis stability: The situation in which, in times of high tension, no country would see any strategic advantage in attacking first with nuclear weapons. The effects of an SDI deployment on crisis stability are presently hard to gauge. Whether the projected defense deployment would lead to crisis stability would depend on the nature of the BMD, the potential effectiveness of civil and air defenses, the number and type of offensive weapons in place, and the perspectives of the political and military leaders.

cruise missile: A winged, jet-propelled, guided nuclear bomb. It can be launched from the land, sea, or air. Because it does not follow a ballistic trajectory, the missile is difficult to detect and defend against, either by the United States or the Soviet Union. However, above-the-horizon radars or sensors, which can pick up targets 1,600 kilometers away, might be used as early-warning devices against cruise missiles. As both sides increase their stocks of such missiles, verification problems may hamper arms control negotiations.

cruise missile (Soviet)

cryocooler: A special miniaturized kind of freezer that would allow the fabrication of long-wave, broad-band, heat-detecting sensors for SDI. The size of a quarter, the cryocooler could cool to 10 degrees Kelvin a niobium nitride superconductor used in germanium infrared detectors. A nonmechanical device pumps the refrigerator fluent; the pump itself is powered from the heat extracted from an outside source.

cryogenic infrared radiation experiment: A test that had been scheduled for the space shuttle before the January 1986 *Challenger* disaster caused its cancelation. It was to have used a supercooled sensor to gather data about the aurora borealis and other natural glows around the earth. It is thought that such radiation can impede the effectiveness of SDI weapons and other technology.

CW: continuous wave.

cyclotron: *See* accelerator, circular.

data processing: SDI components will require extensive computational capabilities. Some are already known but will have to be done faster, while others, such as image interpretation, will require the development of new mathematical and processing techniques. The use of very high-speed integrated circuits is helping to increase the speed of processing, which may be approaching a fundamental limit, but the miniaturization of circuits already may have reached its end. This is leading to the use of parallel processing, in which many processors are tied together to do numerous calculations at once, and to the use of analog devices to process calculations involving laser beams (optical processors). Gallium arsenide holds out the promise of fast and radiation-hard circuits, although these would be larger than the more radiation-sensitive, silicon-based circuits. *See* decentralization; systems analysis/battle management.

dazzling: The overloading of a sensor by an intense signal of electromagnetic radiation such as that from a laser or nuclear explosion. An electro-optical countermeasure that "blinds," or deceives, a sensor.

decentralization: The data processing requirements of a complex SDI system almost certainly will have to be distributed among the many system elements, thereby minimizing the amount of data to be passed from component to component. Such a decentralized architecture could make possible survivable software and hardware systems. For example, a surveillance sensor could process each raw image and then transmit only a simple view of a target to a weapon, rather than the sensor's entire field of view. This would reduce considerably the amount of data transmitted and lessen the risk of system paralysis in the event that the central processor failed.

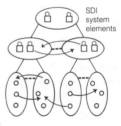

decentralization

decoy: A light object, not containing a warhead, that is designed to look like a nuclear-armed RV. Booster decoys cost one-third to one-half that of an ICBM, but, if a booster fails to fly, the fake boosters are useless. Decoys may weigh less than 1 percent of a warhead. Flight paths of decoys emulate ballistic missile trajectories. They slow down only after entering the atmosphere.

decoy, reaction: A decoy that would be deployed by the defense at the first warning of an impending attack. For instance, a satellite under attack by a pop-up infrared homing interceptor could release lightweight identical decoys which, from a distance, would resemble it in temperature and color.

deep space: The region of outer space 3,000 nautical miles (5,600 kilometers) above the earth's surface.

defense: The complex system designed to deter attack or reduce the damage inflicted in an attack. It operates in three broad categories: active, passive, and preemptive destruction. Each kind of defensive posture may be employed in response to an attack.

defense, active: The defensive posture that seeks to prevent launched weapons from reaching their intended targets. It may make use of ballistic missiles and other air defenses. SDI would be an active defense.

Defense Advanced Research Projects Agency (DARPA): A Department of Defense agency that has developed some of the technology now being explored by the SDIO. It is continuing to explore the potential of the Alpha laser program, which aims at the construction of an HF chemical laser of just a few megawatts for ground-based defense. DARPA, created in 1958, is headed by civilians. It emphasizes research that holds potential for high gains; successful developments are incorporated into the defense establishment.

defense-dominant strategy: A superpower strategy in which defense plays a prominent role, lessening, according to its proponents, the chance of nuclear war and mass destruction. This strategy is viewed as having a moral edge over a retaliatory strategy, which would subject civilians to indiscriminate unleashing of weapons in response to an attack. There remains, however, the problem of deterring a conventional nonnuclear attack. SDI has increased calls for a defense-dominant strategy, but critics argue that it is by no means clear that SDI can be developed, that such a strategy raises the risk of both preemptive nuclear attack and conventional war, and that there is no certainty that a coordinated transition to defense-dominance could ever be carried out. If the Soviet Union and the United States did cooperate in such a transition, likely factors would include the cost-effectiveness of SDI, the total resource base of each country, total defensive-system affordability, the ability to redirect civilian resources to the military, the internal politics of each country, and the relative utility of offensive forces versus defensive forces—that is, the projected ineffectiveness of ICBMs against SDI. *See* arms control policy; net defense capability; transition.

defense industry: More than one-half of all SDI appropriations will go to the big U.S. defense contractors, which are enthusiastic supporters of SDI. Other contractors include the national laboratories and universities. By mid-1986 more than $6 billion already had been awarded to more than 1,300 contractors. The top contractors are Lawrence Livermore National Laboratory ($725 million), GM ($580 million), Lockheed ($520 million), TRW ($350 million), McDonnell Douglas ($350 million), Boeing ($350 million), Los Alamos National Laboratory ($200 million), Rockwell International ($190 million), Teledyne ($180 million), EG&G ($140 million), Gencorp ($130 million), Textron ($90 million), Sandia National Laboratories ($90 million), LTV ($90 million), Flow General ($90 million), Raytheon ($70 million), Science Applications ($70 million), Honeywell ($70 million), Nichols Research ($60 million), and MIT Lincoln Laboratories ($60 million). Other major contractors include Batelle Research Laboratories, Ford Aerospace, GT&E, Grumman, Hughes, IBM (Federal Systems Division), Institute for Defense Analyses (Alexandria, VA), Johns Hopkins University (Applied Physics Lab), Martin Marietta, Naval Research Laboratory, Naval Surface Weapons Center, RCA (Missile Division), Titan Systems, Unisys, and Westinghouse. The overall size of the SDI program could surpass that of the Manhattan Project of World War II. *See* Europe; Great Britain; Japan; West Germany.

Defense Nuclear Agency (DNA): A Department of Defense Agency that has developed some of the technology now being explored in more detail by the SDIO.

defense, passive: A defensive posture that aims to reduce the effectiveness of launched weapons by such nondestructive means as hardening ICBM silos, employing SLBMs, and using conventional nonnuclear forces that are hard to strike. A passive defense might make use of pilotless drones and other unmanned laser-guided craft to resist an attack.

defense, preferential: A hypothetical BMD operating mode in which only selected RVs would be targeted for destruction. The ability to select only those RVs that will do damage may not be entirely feasible, but as a goal it represents the best a BMD could achieve.

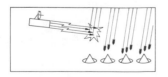
defense, preferential

defense, random subtractive: A BMD operating mode in which the defense shoots at as many RVs as possible, with no attempt being made to distinguish among them. This kind of defense would be characterized by high-kill probabilities or "leakage rates." A random subtractive defense might destroy 90 percent of attacking RVs but still fail to protect population centers or missile silos.

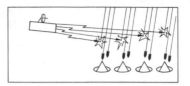

defense, random subtractive

defense, semipreferential: A BMD operating mode in which the defense would shoot at selected RVs, on the basis of previously allocated resources. Thus, such a system might overdefend one area and underdefend another.

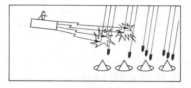

defense, semipreferential

defense suppression: An attempt to overcome a space-based defense system by targeting it for direct attack rather than by making use of a broad range of countermeasures. In December 1986, Mir Publishers in Moscow issued a book emphasizing defense suppression as the means by which the Soviet Union might overcome SDI. Called *Weaponry in Space: The Dilemma of Security*, it was edited by Yevgeny P. Velikhov, vice president of the Academy of Sciences, Andrei Kokoshin, a historian, and Roald Z. Sagdeyev, director of the Space Research Institute. The publication also discusses countermeasures already envisioned by SDIO.

defense suppression

defensive satellite (DSAT): A device intended to defend satellites by destroying ASAT weapons.

defensive technologies study (DTS): A research study by the Fletcher panel, a body of scientists and engineers headed by NASA Administrator James C. Fletcher and appointed by President Ronald Reagan to investigate the potential of BMD systems. In 1983 the fifty members of the group—most of whom worked for the Department of Defense, the national laboratories, or defense contractors—issued a paper on their findings. Entitled "Eliminating the Threat Posed by Nuclear Ballistic Missiles," the report concluded that "the technological challenges of a strategic defense are great but not insurmountable. . . . The United States will reach that point where knowledgeable decisions concerning an engineering validation phase can be made with confidence. The scientific community may indeed give the U.S. the means of rendering the ballistic missile threat impotent and obsolete." The committee members called for a decision by the early 1990s on whether to deploy a BMD system. In January 1984, SDI was established as a research program based on this study.

degradation: The reduced capability to perform a designated job.

DELPHI: *See* discriminating electrons with laser photon ionization.

Delta 180: *See* significant technical milestones (experiment).

Delta 181, 183, 185: A follow-up series of tests to the significant technical milestones (Delta 180) experiment. Delta 181, scheduled for late 1987, will involve the launching of a Delta rocket containing sensors that will track objects in simulation of space-based kinetic-kill targets. The Delta 183, set for September 1988, will be a test of a laser beam directed at a relay mirror. Delta 1985, planned for late 1989, will be a test of the relay mirror called HIBREL.

Delta rocket: A U.S. space launch vehicle that has been used to test SDI experimental programs. In September 1986 it was used in the first major tests of the SATKA project—the significant technical milestones (STM) experiment. The rocket, launched from Cape Canaveral, contained as its payload two satellites that were placed into orbit. One was an ASAT weapon that later destroyed the other satellite at an impact speed of 6,500 miles per hour. The ASAT satellite also carried sensors to observe the booster plume of an Aries rocket launched from White Sands, New Mexico. The Delta rocket was created in 1959 and has gone through several modifications. The current 3900 series is a three-stage rocket, 116 feet tall, that weighs 426,000 pounds at lift-off and develops 631,000 pounds (2,807 kilonewtons) of thrust.

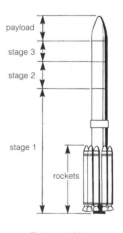

Delta rocket

Delta-V: A numerical index that specifies the maneuverability of a satellite or rocket. It measures the maximum change in velocity that a spacecraft could achieve in the absence of a gravitational field.

demonstration-of-capabilities program: A major program within the SDIO that emphasizes the demonstration of such key SDI systems as the space surveillance and tracking system, the high-endoatmospheric defense interceptor, exoatmospheric reentry-vehicle interceptor subsystem, and the terminal imaging radar.

Department of Energy (DOE): This department is not formally part of SDI, but it does conduct research relevant to the defense program. In 1985 it allocated $2.2 billion for defense-related research and development programs, which included all nuclear weapons research and nuclear studies under joint military/civilian auspices.

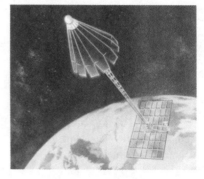

Department of Energy space power (SP-100)

deploy: To place strategically.

deployment: The strategic placement of offensive and defensive weapons. Different approaches on deployment proceed from different sets of assumptions about the value and feasibility of SDI, and the consequences of pursuing SDI research. The chief deployment options are 1) to proceed with SDI research only for the present, 2) to initiate a phased deployment immediately, or 3) to delay deployment indefinitely. The first option—research only—is proposed at present by the Reagan administration, whose aim is to remain in technical compliance with the terms of the ABM Treaty. The immediate deployment approach—favored by conservatives and the Department of Defense—calls for the development of BSTS and SBKKV technology and, in the process, abrogating the treaty and limiting arms control efforts. The third approach—indefinite delay—advocates continued BMD research within the strict bounds of the ABM Treaty, while holding out the possibility of negotiations with the Soviets on agreed force levels with an increased defense role.

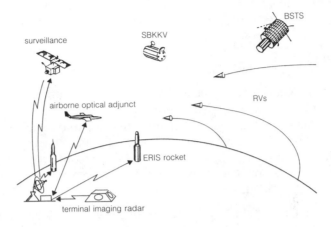

deployment (early): architecture for SDI

Conservatives in the United States, fearful that SDI objectives might be compromised to achieve an arms control agreement, seek immediate phased deployment, the first step of which would be a reactivation of the ABM base in Grand Forks, North Dakota, where 100 interceptors would make use of existing SDI technology. Supporters of this step include Edward Teller, Lowell Wood, Jack Kemp, Alexander Haig, and Eugene Rostow. The Reagan administration could make a decision on near-term deployment of SDI by early 1988. *See* arms control policy; ballistic missile defense; "black program"; functional test vehicle; transition.

detection: The rapid and reliable warning of an attack, and the readying of defenses. Detection includes the ability to maintain full-time worldwide surveillance of ballistic missile launch areas, characterize the composition and size of an attack, determine the offensive target areas, and pass tracking data to other SDI components.

deterrence: The policy of nuclear restraint aimed at discouraging the bilateral use of nuclear force.

deuterium fluoride (DF): A chemical compound of deuterium and fluorine. It is one of a number of compounds used to produce chemical lasers. Deuterium, an isotope of hydrogen, is heavier and more expensive. It can be used to make a DF chemical laser having a wavelength of 3.8 microns. Large mirrors would be needed to make such a laser effective in an SDI system. *See* chemical laser.

DEW: *See* directed-energy weapon.

DF: *See* deuterium fluoride.

dielectric breakdown: A phenomenon that would affect the propogation of a laser through the atmosphere. At radio wavelengths (electromagnetic radiation at wavelengths of 1 millimeter or more), electrons begin to break down, reducing the total energy available to a laser beam. Because of this effect, the maximum pulse energy that could be beamed through the atmosphere is estimated at 1 joule/square meter. *See* laser.

diffraction: The angular spread of a beam, especially a beam of electromagnetic radiation, as it leaves an aperture or a mirror. The degree of spread cannot be eliminated by focusing. Spread is proportional to the ratio of the wavelength of radiation and the diameter of the focusing mirror.

diffraction limit: The minimum angular spread of a beam. The spot size of a laser increases as it moves away from a target. The diffraction limit describes the minimum, or perfect, beam size achieved at the target. A laser with a 1-micrometer (1 micron) wavelength beam, projected by a 1-meter mirror, would have, at best, a 1.2-microradian divergence angle. This could create a 1.2-meter spot on a target 1,000 kilometers away. *See* brightness; divergence angle.

digital processing: The most familiar type of computing, in which problems are solved through the mathematical manipulation of streams of numbers.

direct-ascent interceptor: A ground- or air-launched interceptor or ASAT weapon. It is allowed under the ABM Treaty so long as it is not capable of countering ballistic missiles or their components in space.

directed energy: Focused energy in the form of particles and laser beams that could be transmitted over long distances at the speed of light. A particle beam is a stream of subatomic particles. *See* directed-energy weapon; laser; particle beam.

directed-energy weapon (DEW): A weapon that would destroy targets by delivering energy at or near the speed of light. Also called beam weapons, they include chemical lasers, excimer and free-electron beams, particle beam weapons, and microwave generators. Beam weapons are being considered for use in intercepting boost-phase ICBMs and discriminating between midcourse decoys and warheads in SDI. So far, however, DEWs and other devices with applications in boost-phase intercept have not yet been built in the laboratory. Should researchers succeed, they would still need to design such devices in a form suitable for incorporation in a complete defense system. Nevertheless, the SDIO has made these hypothetical weapons the focus of its efforts. It reports that work with atmospheric compensation and free-electron laser technologies has progressed to the point where the potential for a large and effective ground-based laser is very real.

The chief advantage of such a weapon would be its speed. Its ability to deliver killing energy at or near the speed of light means it would arrive at the target in less than 1/10 of a second. Such speed also would be the key to overcoming fast-burn boosters. There are three types of kill mechanisms by which directed-energy systems act. *See* functional kill; impulse kill; thermal kill.

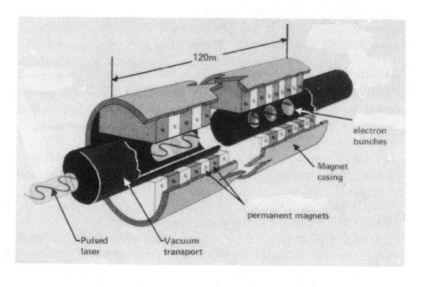

directed-energy weapon (free-electron laser)

directed-energy weapons (DEW) program: The SDI research effort that is investigating space-based lasers (SBL), ground-based lasers (GBL), space-based particle beams (SBPB), and nuclear-directed energy weapons (NDEW). Research necessarily encompasses high-powered laser and particle beam generators; optics and sensors to direct and control the high-power beams; the use of large yet light-weight mirrors and magnets to focus the beams; the acquisition, tracking, and pointing of the beams; and fire control of the beams to the targets. These research efforts have been consolidated by SDIO into four projects: 1) technology-base development, 2) technology-integration experiments, 3) concept formulation and technology-development planning, and 4) design support programs. The six major experiments in this program are Alpha/LODE/LAMP, MIRACL, ATP, GBFEL, HIBREL, and NPB.

discriminating electrons with laser photon ionization (DELPHI): Sandia Laboratory's research program in target discrimination. DELPHI is to be a pop-up system that would use a laser beam to weigh and sort decoys in late midcourse and terminal phases of a BMD. It could be used for high-value targets as a short-range discriminator, first augmenting the passive airborne optical adjunct (AOA), and then replacing the AOA as its capability decreased. In 1987 the SDIO reduced funding requests for this long-term program.

discrimination: The ability of a surveillance system to distinguish decoys from real warheads and targets. Discrimination would be a critical task of any layered SDI system. The discrimination of actual missiles, buses, and warheads from nonthreatening decoys and other debris would rely on the use of sensors and a variety of measures to overcome, among other things, spoofing, hiding, antisimulation, and simulation. These measures would note changes in RV velocities, electromagnetic emissions, the rate of temperature changes of objects, the characteristics of rocket plumes, and other phenomena of observed targets.

The SDIO reports progress in imaging due to improvements in phased-array radar technology and signal processing. Its efforts in directed energy have led to "interactive" discrimination, the reading of signatures from warheads in space. Active sensors, which could measure body dynamics and the size and shape of objects during and after deployment, appear to offer the best promise for discrim-

ination. High-powered DEWs with fast retarget times could be used
as backups to destroy penetration aids or decoys, but neutral particle
beams would require the use of many radiation-detection sensors
for interactive discrimination.

discrimination, interactive: A surveillance system's ability to differentiate between warheads and decoys by transmitting neutral particle beams to detect the emission of gamma rays. Only the warheads
would emit such radiation. SDI's goals for neutral particle beam
(NPB) research were reoriented in 1986 to emphasize interactive
discrimination. SDI scientists envision an NPB device that would
tap warheads and decoys, and a nearby detector device that would
pick up neutron and gamma-ray emissions. Building a prototype
model of an NPB accelerator and detector requires significant advances in engineering and physics. The weight of the space-based
accelerator and detector must be reduced from 300 metric tons to
30, according to scientists at Los Alamos National Laboratory. In
addition, current accelerators take weeks to start up and then constantly must be fine-tuned by technicians. There also are the other
problems of piecing the system together and then providing it with
power. Scientists at Sandia National Laboratory do not envision a
workable NPB system before the year 2000.

divergence angle: The angle at which directed energy is focused. The
smaller the angle (expressed in radians), the more intense is the
beam spot. However, there is a limit to how small the divergence
angle for a laser can be; it can be no smaller than 1.2 times the
wavelength of the light divided by the diameter of the focusing
mirror. In a neutral particle beam (NPB), the divergence angle is
created by the stripping of electrons from a collection of negative
hydrogen or tritium ions. According to the Heisenberg uncertainty
principle, the production of this angle is an unavoidable conse-
quence. Even if an accelerator of negative ions were absolutely
perfect, there would still be a divergence angle. For a laser beam,
with a wavelength of 2.7 microns, the divergence angle would
conceivably permit a lethal beam to be projected with a 10-meter
mirror onto an ICBM booster at 3,000 kilometers if the amount of
energy were equal to 15 kilojoules/square (or cubic) centimeters for
3.5 seconds.

	NPB Divergence Angles (microradians)	
	Hydrogen	Tritium
100MeV	3.6	2.0
500MeV	1.4	1.0

divert: To maneuver. The term is used when speaking of KEW propulsion.

DNA: *See* Defense Nuclear Agency.

doctrines: The amalgam of experience, theoretical principles, technical capabilities, detailed understanding of morale and motivational factors, and guesswork that governs the use of military forces by the United States and the Soviet Union. It is generally accepted as better to have doctrines, even imperfect ones, than to operate without them, and important to develop a sound doctrine for military operations in space. Two central facts could influence the development of U.S. doctrines governing warfare in space: 1) The arsenal of weapons designed to shoot down satellites is likely to be more effective than the means to defend them because a lower level of technology is needed; and 2) the coastal locations of key U.S. launch sites—Cape Canaveral, Florida; Wallops Island, Virginia; and Vandenberg Air Force Base, California—make them vulnerable to attack.

Some SDI proponents envision the in-ground storage of satellites for wartime use only after orbiting military satellites have been attacked. This would require two sets of military satellite systems: one for peacetime and the other designed to survive wartime, even a nuclear exchange. The wartime system—SDI—would have to be launched from protected sites within the continental United States.

DOD: Department of Defense.

DOE: *See* Department of Energy.

dog: Military slang for a ballistic missile.

dog house: The battle-management radar that is part of the Soviet ABM system around Moscow. *See* Soviet Union.

Drell, Sidney: Deputy director of the Stanford Linear Accelerator Center in California. An outspoken critic of SDI, he argues that the proposed system is not technologically feasible. Drell is coauthor of "The Reagan Strategic Defense Initiative: A Technical, Political, and Arms Control Assessment" (1984).

DSAT: *See* defensive satellite.

DTS: *See* defensive technologies study.

dwell time: The amount of time a laser beam must be fixed on a point in order to deliver enough energy to destroy a target, either by thermal kill or impulse kill. The estimated dwell time for a 20-megawatt HF chemical laser with a wavelength of 2.7 microns and a range of 4,000 meters is calculated at 7 seconds. *See* 10-kilojoule criterion.

dynamic reconfiguration: The alteration of defense plans by a battle-management system to respond to changing circumstances.

Dynamics Research: A military contractor headquartered in Wilmington, Massachusetts. This corporation is involved in the determination, research, and analysis of potential SDI architectures.

e

early warning: The almost immediate detection of an enemy's launching of ballistic missiles through the use of satellites and long-range radars. The latter instruments are a source of dispute between the United States and the Soviet Union because the construction of new radars, except under certain conditions, is prohibited by the ABM Treaty. Some observers have voiced concern that the United States may be violating the treaty by "modernizing" two early-warning radars in Greenland and Britain—replacing them with phased-array radars—while the USSR is constructing a phased-array radar in Abalakova in central Siberia. The USSR has offered to scrap its new radar if the United States will do likewise, but the offer has been refused. *See* ABM Treaty; phased-array radar; Soviet Union.

Eastport Study Group: The name of the group created in 1984 by the SDIO to investigate the requirements of computer support for battle-management systems. In 1985 the group, headed by Professor Daniel Cohen of the University of Southern California, provided a list of problems that the SDIO would have to resolve in order to create meaningful battle-management programs. The findings did not satisfy critics of SDI. *See* battle management.

echoes: Radar signals reflected from targets. The energy of radar returns from an orbiting target cannot be detected by rapidly scanning the sky. Only if the target position is known can the radar successfully scan in that general direction, accumulating signals over a period of time.

educators and educational institutions: About 6,500 American scientists and teachers have signed petitions opposing SDI research or refusing to accept SDI funding. Some institutions also have gone on record against SDI, but Johns Hopkins, UCLA, MIT, and others are participating. *See* innovative science and technology program.

efficiency: The ratio of the energy pumped into a system to the energy released. Conventional lasers convert only a small proportion of the power transmitted to them into laser light. Therefore, very little of the energy used to produce the laser beam actually can be applied to destroying military targets. Although beams of fairly high intensity—from several hundred kilowatts to perhaps 1 megawatt—have been produced, the instruments capable of creating them require large and complex installations. Some experimental laser models, such as free-electron lasers, have much higher energy conversion ratios. The efficiency of the free-electron laser, for instance, is now about 20 percent. For other kinds of lasers, it is only a few percent. *See* free-electron laser.

electromagnetic accelerator: *See* electromagnetic railgun.

electromagnetic pulse (EMP): The electromagnetic shock wave produced by a nuclear explosion, which destroys electronic and computer circuitry. Discovered by the United States in 1962, EMP has the potential to be used as a weapon, thereby destroying complex technological systems at the speed of light.

electromagnetic radiation: A form of propagated energy, arising from electric charges in motion, that produces a simultaneous wavelike variation of electric and magnetic fields in space. The highest frequencies (or shortest wavelengths) of such radiation belong to gamma rays, which originate from processes within atomic nuclei. At lower frequencies, the electromagnetic spectrum includes X-rays, ultraviolet light, infrared light, microwaves, and radio waves. The shorter the wavelength, the more powerful the laser. For instance, an X-ray laser with a wavelength of 0.1 nanometers (1 angstrom) would be highly efficient.

electromagnetic railgun: A huge KEW that would use electromagnetic forces rather than explosions to "shoot" projectiles. It would do this by using an electromagnetic accelerator with an intense

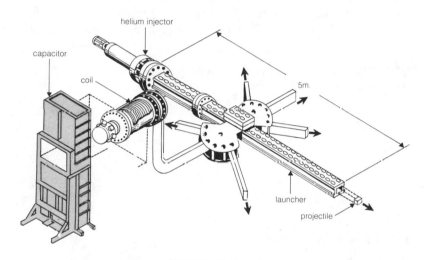

electromagnetic railgun

magnetic field to impart great velocities to electrically conducting projectiles. The conducting substance can be formed by ionizing a material that normally might be an insulator, thereby producing speeds of more than 20 kilometers/second. However, accelerations of hundreds of thousands of times that of gravity would be needed for SDI's purposes. The weapon's range might be 1,600 kilometers, but it would require large power sources for every shot, enough to power a small town. The railgun also would need to deliver energy in short pulses; depend on guidance systems that can survive rapid accelerations; and have proven accuracy, good recoil momentum, and refiring capabilities.

SDI researchers have demonstrated the ability to obtain high levels of power for these devices sooner than expected. This advance moves the United States closer to having the capability to fire heavier projectiles at higher than previously attainable speeds. SDI's IST program has developed operating specifications for an electromagnetic launcher that can accelerate 100-gram projectiles to 5 kilometers/second, with a duty cycle of twenty shots per week. Data from this program will be used to test new rail materials and insulators.

electromagnetic railgun, land-based: One of three SDI research programs that will evaluate kinetic-energy technology. This program aims to demonstrate launchings of guided and unguided projectiles from a railgun. The testing of a railgun in a laboratory or in a fixed ground-based mode at a BMD test range is permissible according to the 1972 ABM Treaty.

electromagnetic railgun, space-based: A major SDI research program to investigate the potential of a space-based railgun system to defend against ASAT interceptors. In connection with this, SDI researchers are studying hypervelocity and repetitively pulsed railguns with "smart" bullets.

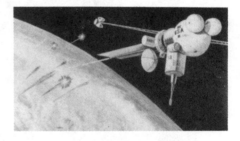

electromagnetic railgun, space-based

electron volt (eV): The energy gained by an electron in passing through a potential difference of 1 volt. One eV expresses the energy of each accelerated ion in a neutral particle beam; it is equal to 1 watt per ampere. Multiplying the current by the energy gives the power of a neutral particle beam; therefore, a 1-ampere beam of 100 MeV particles carries 100 megawatts of power. *See* neutral particle beam.

electronic beam: Another type of nonbending beam, apart from the neutral particle beam, that physical theory holds possible. According to the theory it could be produced only under certain circumstances, in the thin air of near-earth space. A laser beam would have to remove all air molecules in a channel from a battle station to a target. Into the resulting

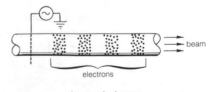

electronic beam

channel of free electrons and positive ions would be injected a high-energy, high-current electronic beam. The beam's electrons would repel the free electrons, and the positive ions would work to prevent the bending of the beam itself because of the geomagnetic field. The effect of the electronic beam on any target would theoretically resemble that of a neutral particle beam.

electronic intelligence (ELINT): The detection of radar emissions by military satellites.

electronic support measure (ESM): Part of a military signal intelligence collections system that performs direction-finding or signal interception from the ground. One example of an ESM is a passive sensor used for deep-space detection.

ELINT: *See* electronic intelligence.

ELINT ocean reconnaissance satellite: Military satellite that detects, locates, and classifies ships according to the radio signals emitted by their communications and radar systems. This kind of satellite is usually positioned 250 to 425 kilometers above the earth.

elliptical orbit: A noncircular Keplerian orbit.

emission: The process by which an atom or molecule loses energy. The term is frequently applied to radiation.

emission, spontaneous: The emission of photons by an atom or molecule without outside or artificial stimulus.

emission, stimulated: The emission of photons facilitated by the presence of other artificially introduced photons. Emission produces photons; absorption consumes them.

emissivity: A target's ability to emit heat by radiation; a ratio of a target's emitted radiant energy to a black body's emitted energy at the same temperature. SDI applications require emissivity studies in such areas as ballistic missile signatures and the determining, modeling, and controlling of infrared emissivity. *See* sensor.

EMP: *See* electromagnetic pulse.

EMRLD: An SDI-developed excimer laser that would use pulsed waves rather than continuous waves to achieve greater lethality.

enclave defense: A defensive posture by a neutral particle beam weapon in which a cluster of distant satellites would be protected from coorbital or direct-ascent interceptors or continuous-wave lasers.

encryption: The encoding of electronically transmitted signals, such as those for a missile's test flight or a weapons system, so that other nations are not aware that the test is being monitored. Encoded data would include the speed of a missile, its acceleration, the temperatures of rocket fuels, and fuel consumption per second. Under SALT II the United States and the Soviet Union may not use encryption when it will "impede verification" of treaty adherence. Radar can pick up information such as the number of RVs; other critical data, such as the number of rocket stages, launch weights, and throw-weights, are to remain unimpeded according to the treaty.

END: *See* European nuclear disarmament.

end game: The high-speed, accurate, and reliable interceptor needed to make space-based kinetic-kill vehicles workable. SBKKV contractors and project managers assert that this is the biggest hurdle they face in developing kill vehicles.

endoatmospheric: Within the atmosphere.

engagement time: The amount of time a weapon takes to destroy a target. Engagement time includes firing time plus the time needed for instruments to accommodate to a particular target.

Environmental Modification Convention: The international agreement reached in 1980 to prohibit any changes to the dynamics, composition, or structure of earth or outer space through manipulation of natural processes.

EORSAT: ELINT ocean reconnaissance satellite.

ephemeris: Any collection of data about predicted or apparent positions of celestial objects, including artificial satellites. A satellite's ephemeris might contain the orbital parameters of satellites and anticipated future changes in their position.

equity standards: Ceilings, relative reductions, and absolute reductions in nuclear forces between parties to an arms control agreement.

ERINT: *See* extended range interceptor.

ERIS: *See* exoatmospheric reentry-vehicle interceptor subsystem.

EUREKA: *See* European Research Coordination Agency.

Europe: The Continent's stance toward SDI is split, with France, Denmark, and Norway opposing involvement in SDI research programs, and West Germany, Great Britain, and Italy seeking to join. Some Europeans favor a more self-sufficient approach such as a European defense initiative (EDI) or a civilian research program like EUREKA. Meanwhile, more than twenty-five SDI contracts already have been given to European organizations. These include in Britain: the Ministry of Defense, Atomic Energy Authority, General Electric, Harriet Watts University, Rutherford Appleton Laboratory, and Logica; in West Germany: Messerschmitt-Bolkow-Blohm, Dornier, Interatom, Schott Optical Glass, and Carl Zeiss; in France: Thomson CSF; and in Italy: Selenia Electronics Company and Fiat. In December 1986 the SDIO awarded $2-million contracts to each of seven U.S.-European consortia (twenty-nine European and twenty-two U.S. firms were represented) to develop studies for the theater defense of Europe. The European teams are headed by SNIA BPB in Italy, Messerschmitt-Bolkow-Blohm in West Germany, and Aerospatiale and Thomson CSF in France. European organizations are expected to receive more than $300 million in SDI contracts by 1990.

European defense: If SDI bolsters the defense of the superpowers only, some observers say, Europe would be left more vulnerable to nuclear attack for several reasons. First, the layered-defense architecture of SDI will not apply entirely to short-range systems threatening Europe. Second, since the trajectories of some short-range systems from the Soviet Union are designed not to leave the atmosphere, they would be vulnerable to attack by boost-phase and terminal-phase interception only, although the boost-phase layer will be the most difficult to achieve under SDI. Third, tactical and theater-range systems threatening Europe are less likely to contain multiple RVs, thereby lessening the advantages of destroying them in a boost-phase intercept. Their warheads, on the other hand, would move toward their targets more slowly than would ICBM warheads, so they might be vulnerable to some kind of terminal defense. But, since there would be no midcourse defense, there would be no discrimination data available for the terminal defense. Finally, other delivery systems—bombers, cruise missiles, artillery, and even mines—can be used against Europe with impunity as far as SDI is concerned. Accordingly, some argue that an SDI system is not the answer to defending the Continent. Nonetheless, in late 1986 the SDIO asked for bids from U.S. and European firms for architectures that would define a theater-level defense for Europe against tactical and cruise missiles. *See* architecture; horserace acquisition studies.

European nuclear disarmament (END): A London-based movement opposed to SDI. It advocates finding political solutions to obviate the need for nuclear arms.

European Research Coordination Agency (Eureka): A civilian alternative to SDI proposed in 1985 by President François Mitterrand of France. A seventeen-nation, high-technology program, it will emphasize work in lasers, particle beams, supercomputers, microelectronics, artificial intelligence, optical switching, robotics, and biotechnology. Critics have called it a hollow shell, a way of trying to kill off the SDI program and to force West Germany, still fence-straddling, to choose between SDI and EUREKA. Others view EUREKA more favorably as a program designed to enable Europe to master advanced technologies. The laser project, for instance, calls for Britain, France, Italy, and West Germany to research the excimer laser.

eV: *See* electron volt.

Excalibur device: An X-ray laser under study by the United States about which little has been disclosed. *See* X-ray laser.

excimer: An excited dimer, or two-atom molecule, typically consisting of a noble gas (argon, krypton, xenon) atom and a halogen (chlorine, fluorine) atom. Some dimers—xenon chloride and krypton fluoride—are molecules that cannot exist under ordinary conditions because they do not form stable molecules in the ground state. These must be created in an excited, or energized, condition by the special pumping processes of lasers.

excimer laser: The light-producing laser created by the decay of dimers from an excited upper state to a lower level. In an excited state—produced by a pulsed electrical discharge, rather than by a continuous chemical reaction—these two-atom molecules form a bound molecular system, but, when the molecules drop to a ground state, they separate into individual atoms, giving off photons of light. This light occurs in pulses, and, after each pulse of radiation, the light-producing process can be repeated. Although the pumping process is complex and inefficient, the comparatively short wavelength of excimer lasers, compared to that of HF chemical lasers, makes them valued. A typical excimer laser wavelength is 0.3 to 0.5 microns in the near-ultraviolet to visible region of the spectrum. In addition, mirrors only 1/10 the size (1/100 the area) of those for chemical lasers would be needed to reflect the beam toward a target. However, while an excimer's aiming mirror might be only about 15 meters in diameter, the optical requirements to keep the beam down to 1 meter in diameter at 40,000 kilometers would be more stringent than for other lasers.

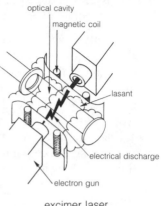

excimer laser

In a ground-based defensive scheme, the excimer laser, even at short wavelengths, would have to be very powerful to travel through the atmosphere and bounce off two mirrors while still retaining lethality. Great power—hundreds of megawatts— large relay mirrors, and the use of adaptive optics might permit ground-basing. Since the laser would have a high weight-to-output power ratio, space-basing seems out of the question. At present, however, the development of the excimer laser is at an early stage. No excimer lasers exist with anything remotely approaching the characteristics needed for boost-phase intercept. Power outputs achieved in the laboratory are smaller than the average power needed for thermal kill, and the energy achieved in a single pulse is much smaller than that required for impulse kill.

The laser thus far also has not been able to attain the light weight necessary to make use of the weapon practical. Still, SDI has generated a near-diffraction-limited beam on a single-pulse basis, whose beam quality reduces the power required from the device for possible GBLs. A process called Raman conversion might lead to more powerful but longer wavelength excimer lasers. Also, advances in high-power electrical pulse conditioning; high-efficiency, large-area electron guns; and acoustic damping have given the SDIO more confidence in the potential of excimer laser technology. *See* ground-based laser; Raman conversion.

excitation: The source of energy that helps achieve a population inversion in atoms. The number of atoms that have absorbed photons exceeds those at lower energy levels. This imbalance is necessary to achieve light amplification and lasing. The means of excitation causes most of the atoms in an active medium to reach the excited state from which they emit photons through stimulated emission. *See* laser.

exoatmospheric: Outside the atmosphere. An exoatmospheric interceptor reaches its target in space.

exoatmospheric reentry-vehicle interceptor subsystem (ERIS): The major SDI experimental program that is looking at the possibilities of intercepting ballistic missile warheads above the atmosphere. ERIS is SDI's most mature interceptor technology. In 1984 the U.S. Army successfully tested a heat-seeking interceptor, traveling at 6 kilometers/second, which hit a dummy warhead launched 6,200 kilometers away. Future planned test flights include the launching of the first stage of a rocket, the launching of all stages without homing devices, homing against a point in space, and hit-to-kill against targets. Fixed systems will be capable of launching only one interceptor missile at a time—with a range of 4,000 kilometers—and will not be rapidly reloadable. The integration experiments intended to tie in ERIS, HEDI, and the TIR have been canceled due to lack of funding by SDIO. Lockheed is the manufacturer of the interceptor missile to be used in this series of experiments. For the interceptor to be workable, it must be "cheap" ($1–$2 million) and have a lightweight front end. *See* functional test vehicle.

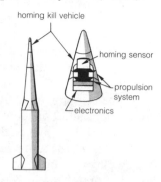

homing kill vehicle

homing sensor

propulsion system

electronics

exoatmospheric reentry-vehicle interceptor subsystem

extended range interceptor (ERINT): A modified version of the projectile used in the three flexible lightweight agile-guided experiments (FLAGE) conducted by the U.S. Army in 1986. It will be more powerful and make use of a nonnuclear fused warhead in tests against tactical missiles.

f

fast-burn booster: A ballistic missile that can burn out much more quickly than current versions, possibly before leaving the atmosphere entirely. Such rapid burnout would complicate any boost-phase defense. *See* booster.

Federation of American Scientists: An organization of scientists who oppose SDI, based in Washington, DC.

FEL: *See* free-electron laser.

first-strike action: The situation in which either the United States or the Soviet Union, fearing that its retaliatory capabilities were about to be lost or greatly reduced, supposed the other side were about to attack. This kind of situation could stimulate reactive offensive and defensive deployments of ICBMs, sea-based SLBMs, bombers, cruise missiles, and strategic moves in air defenses.

fission: The breaking apart of the nucleus of an atom, usually by means of a neutron. For very heavy elements, the process releases an enormous amount of energy. The controlled release of energy generated by this process has civilian use, including commercial electric generation. The rapid uncontrolled release of this type of energy has great destructive power, such as that contained in uranium- and plutonium-based nuclear weapons. Fission also provides the trigger for fusion weapons. *See* X-ray laser.

Fletcher, James C.: NASA administrator who led a scientific panel in 1983 which called for a six-year, $1.5-billion effort to develop a BMD system. It would make use of third-generation nuclear weapons. *See* defensive technologies study.

flexible lightweight agile-guided experiment (FLAGE): A series of nine SDI experiments intended to demonstrate the use of KEWs for terminal interception of RVs. The prime contractor of the experiments is the LTV Aerospace and Defense Company in Dallas. The KEW in these experiments is a projectile 12 feet long, guided by 216 solid rocket motors. It has its own radar and computer system. *See* ERINT.

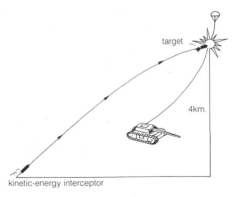

flexible lightweight agile-guided experiment

flexible response: The hypothetical strategy describing a so-called small-scale initial use of nuclear weapons against an enemy, with the hope of avoiding escalation to a large-scale nuclear exchange. This has been hinted at as a plan for first use of nuclear weapons by the United States against the Soviet Union.

fluence: The amount of energy per unit area on a target. *See* 10-kilojoule criterion.

footprint: The area that would be defended by an interceptor missile in a terminal defense.

force-multiplication factors: Also referred to as force multipliers, the value military satellites have in increasing the effectiveness of forces in a particular situation. For instance, the use of navigational satellites may improve the accuracy with which munitions can be delivered, thus reducing waste. In this case the satellites would be considered force-multiplication factors for the munitions systems. These factors have led some to reassess the significance of ASAT weapons in terms of the additional forces the United States would need if it could not use military satellites.

Ford Aerospace & Communications: A military contractor located in Colorado Springs. Its SDI contracts involve work on boost-phase, midcourse, and terminal-phase interception, including battle-management contracts with both the U.S. Army and Air Force.

forward-based weapons: Those U.S. nuclear weapons deployed on carrier-based warplanes and on planes and missiles located in Europe and closer to the Soviet Union than are U.S. land-based systems.

fragment cloud: A cluster of small objects placed in front of a target in space. The cluster would make the target easier to identify and destroy.

France: Although France has not signed any formal agreements with the United States that would encourage its companies to be involved in SDI research programs, at least one French firm—Thomson CSF—has received a $1.2-million contract to furnish free-electron laser components for the SDI program. *See* Europe.

fratricide: The unintentional destruction of one's own forces from the effects of nuclear weapons.

freedom to mix: The agreed right to vary nuclear force compositions under negotiated constraints.

free-electron laser (FEL): The lasant or light-emitter formed by charged

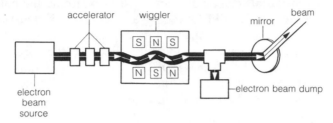

free-electron laser

particles emitted from a particle accelerator. When the paths of these charged particles are then bent by a magnetic field, they oscillate and emit radiation, which is then "free" to be "tuned" to any wavelength. The FEL is a recent development. Its beams of electrons are passed through a periodically varying magnetic field called a wiggler or undulator. The radiation then produced is an intense coherent laser beam, in which the interaction of the electrons and the magnetic field replaces the energy levels of a lasant as the source of coherent radiation. The wavelength—dependent only on the periodicity of the magnetic field and on the electrons' energy—can be changed by varying either condition. Thus the electrons are free and not bound to specific upper- and lower-energy levels. Theoretically, the FEL can produce or amplify wavelengths from infrared to ultraviolet. (FEL operations have been demonstrated at microwave frequencies at the Lawrence Livermore National Laboratory, but the technology needs to be extended to produce a visible wavelength laser. At Los Alamos National Laboratory, FEL operations were achieved in the near-infrared.)

In an SDI architecture the FEL, operating in the visible wavelength range—SDI favors a 1-micron wavelength—would be ground-based. Space-based mirrors would enable it to reach targets beyond the horizon. Higher energy efficiencies and greatly reduced size would have to be achieved to permit space-basing of the laser. The laser's advantages are good beam quality and high-energy efficiencies (now about 20 percent, compared to just a few percent for chemical lasers). However, it is subject to thermal blooming and scattering of the beam when it hits the atmosphere. Still, the technology is in its infancy, and, while high power, beam quality, and efficiency have not been demonstrated, the SDI program is investigating whether power levels can be increased at more useful wavelengths and, as in the case of excimer lasers, whether window and mirror materials can be developed. It is exploring the potential of radio frequency-type FELs (being tested by TRW and Boeing) that use accelerator cavities made of niobium, a superconductor that might improve efficiency considerably. Because the FEL is now among the favored boost-phase DEWs for SDI, a $1-billion laser facility is being built at the White Sands Missile Range in New Mexico. *See* ground-based free-electron laser.

FTV: *See* functional test vehicle.

functional kill: The disabling of a target or target components by DEWs. The resulting damage may not be immediately detectable, but it is serious enough to prevent the target from functioning properly. Also called a soft kill because it can incapacitate a target without obliterating it, a functional kill might entail the crippling of a guidance system's electronics by neutral particle beams or microwave weapons.

Effects of Particle Beams	
Functional Kill (ICBM)	*Energy Deposited (joules/gm)*
Electronics	0.01–10.0
Detonation of propellants	200
Softening of uranium, plutonium	100s
Aluminum melting	1,000

functional test vehicle (FTV): A vehicle twice the size of the operational ERIS interceptor SDIO wants Lockheed to produce. Following FTV tests, SDIO would make a full-scale engineering decision concerning ERIS in 1993. ERIS would then have an initial operational capability at about 1998 and a full operational capability by the year 2000. If SDI were to be deployed by 1994, a version of the FTV—100 interceptors—would be deployed at the Safeguard site at Grand Forks, North Dakota, by 1992, according to Lockheed. The ten-year life cycle cost of the deployment would be $3.5 billion.

fusion: The combining of atomic nuclei, usually of light elements such as hydrogen. Enormous energy is liberated in the process. Hydrogen bombs produce most of their energy through the fusion of hydrogen and helium.

g

gallium arsenide: A compound of arsenic and gallium that shows promise for making faster and more radiation-resistant circuits than those based on silicon. Only the United States and Japan produce this compound for computer chips.

Galosh: The Soviet ICBM interceptor that is part of the ABM system around Moscow. This terminal-phase defense system is believed to contain perhaps 100 Galosh launchers, according to the U.S. Department of Defense. *See* Soviet Union.

Galosh ABM interceptor

gamma-ray laser: A hypothetical laser that would generate gamma rays; also referred to as a graser. It would have higher energy levels and a shorter wavelength than the X-ray laser but would not depend on fission or fusion to produce a beam. Instead, it would be charged on the ground and sent into space, where it could conceivably remain beam-ready for years. The materials from which such a device would be made have not yet been identified, and some believe such a device will never have military potential.

Garwin, Richard: IBM fellow at the Thomas J. Watson Research Center in New York. An expert on space weapons, Garwin was the designer of the trigger mechanism for the hydrogen bomb. He opposes SDI, claiming such a system is unfeasible.

gauge of nuclear capability: The ratio of weapons to targets. This measure of military strength is of interest to participants in an arms control agreement.

GBFEL: *See* ground-based free-electron laser.

GBHRG: *See* ground-based hypervelocity railgun.

GBL: *See* ground-based laser.

GBMD: *See* global ballistic missile defense.

GEODSS: *See* ground-based, electro-optical deep-space surveillance.

George C. Marshall Institute: A conservative "think tank" (located in Washington, DC) that issued the 1986 report, "Deployment of Missile Defenses in the 1990s." Authored by John Gardner, Edward Gerry, Robert Jastrow, William Nierenberg, and Frederick Seitz, the paper stressed that SDI could be deployed fully by 1994, if the decision to deploy were made in 1987. The BMD system would cost $121 billion (how that figure is arrived at is not explained) and make extensive use of space-based kinetic-kill vehicles (11,000) and ground-based interceptors (13,000) against a "threat cloud" of 10,000 warheads and 100,000 decoys. Gardner, Gerry, and Nierenberg were members of the Defensive Technologies Study Team.

geostationary orbit: An orbit of 35,800 kilometers above the equator. A satellite in such an orbit can be made to revolve around the earth once per day, maintaining the same position relative to the planet. This position may be used as a communications relay or surveillance post.

geosynchronous orbit: *See* geostationary orbit.

GLCM: ground-launched cruise missile.

global ballistic missile defense (GBMD): A concept put forth by the High Frontier Program. It would use rocket-propelled interceptors for boost-phase intercept. In order to have surveillance and tracking for its space-based KEWs, GBMD calls for 432 satellites (twenty-four planes of eighteen satellites) at 600 kilometers. However, all these satellites would still provide only meager coverage of Soviet ICBM fields and no capability against an MX-like booster, which would burn out before any interceptor could reach it. Even for postboost-phase intercept, this kind of system could provide only partial coverage. *See* High Frontier Program.

Graham, Lt. Gen. Daniel O.: Director, High Frontier Program (promoting early deployment of SDI), adviser to President Ronald Reagan, and former head of the Defense Intelligence Agency.

graser: Gamma-ray amplification by stimulated emission of radiation. *See* gamma-ray laser.

gray (gy): A unit of absorbed ionizing radiation. One unit is the equivalent of 1 joule of absorbed energy per kilogram of matter. Doses of 100 grays would probably upset the electronic circuits of most satellites. The circuits could be shielded, but the mass of the shielding would be too great to be feasible. However, it is possible to fabricate integrated circuits that are capable of withstanding radiation doses of 100 kilograys. Low-density gallium arsenide circuits, which can withstand such doses, have been fabricated, as have higher density silicon circuits. *See* Sandia National Laboratories.

Great Britain: This nation favors participation in SDI research programs. British companies and organizations already have received $30 million in contracts for work. These include $10 million to the Ministry of Defense to study the architecture of a tactical European BMD system and to research lethality, target hardening, battle management, electromagnetic railgun design, and countermeasures; $4.3 million to the Atomic Energy Authority to research neutral particle beam weapons; $2 million to General Electric to study battle management; $2 million to Harriet Watts University (with Ferranti) to study the technology of optical switching; and $2 million to Logica to create programs for battle management.

ground-based, electro-optical deep-space surveillance (GEODSS): A telescopic system of sensors operated by the U.S. Air Force as part of its space detection and tracking system (SPADATS). Components of the surveillance systems are located in New Mexico, South Korea, Hawaii, the island of Diego Garcia, and Portugal.

ground-based free-electron laser (GBFEL): A major DEW experiment of SDI (formerly the ground-based laser uplink) that will devise a high-power laser to examine the effects of the atmosphere on beam propagation. A spacecraft will measure beam properties, and all work will conform to the ABM Treaty. The SDIO, which now seems to favor the free-electron laser (FEL) over the chemical laser, is looking at two approaches to accelerating the electron beam of the laser: the radio frequency linear accelerator (linac), which uses microwaves sent into the waveguide cavity to speed up the beam; and the induction linear accelerator, which makes use of transformers to speed up the beam. The first approach is being tested by Los Alamos National Laboratory, Boeing, TRW, and Stanford University. The latter is being tested by Lawrence Livermore National Laboratory. Both types of FELs would be pulsed, but the induction-type FEL also would have a very high-intensity output. The lethality of the radio frequency linac FEL resembles that of the chemical laser with its continuous-wave beam.

A $1-billion GBFEL facility will be built at the White Sands Missile Range in New Mexico by 1994. At present, it is expected to accommodate an induction-type FEL, whose efficiency is higher. The FEL will be 1 mile long and will include an electron accelerator (2,400 feet long) and a wiggler (660 feet long) to convert the electron energy to laser radiation. A vacuum tunnel will allow the beam to spread without damaging the mirrors. SDI researchers hope to produce an FEL with a near-infrared wavelength of 1 micron. The site itself will be about 3 square miles, with a target-calibration range 6 miles away.

ground-based hypervelocity railgun (GBHRG): A major KEW experiment of SDI that, while not yet fully defined, is intended to validate the use of these kinds of projectiles. This test will not constitute a violation of the ABM Treaty, according to the SDIO.

ground-based laser (GBL): A laser stationed on earth, whose beams would be bounced off mirrors in space to attack ascending boosters. This scheme avoids placing the laser and its power supply in space, although mirrors, aiming equipment, and sensors would remain. The excimer and the free-electron lasers are possible candidates for ground-basing. These lasers would emit light—at visible or ultraviolet wavelengths—that would be ten times shorter than the near-infrared wavelengths of the chemical laser in a space-based architecture. The shorter wavelengths would require the use of smaller, more finely machined mirrors. Producing a GBL will be a monumental undertaking for the SDIO, which must build a device to make the laser, as well as to construct the beam director that receives the laser and prepares it for passage through the atmosphere.

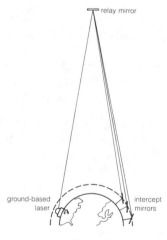

ground-based laser

The high power available with ground-basing would favor impulse rather than thermal kill. However, only about 1/10 of the power emitted by a GBL could be focused on a booster; the remaining 9/10 would be lost to the atmosphere, or dispersed by the relay and battle mirrors. Therefore, if 10 kilojoules/cubic centimeter are required to destroy a target, calculations indicate that 40 megawatts of power must be reflected from the intercept mirror. Thus, a 400-megawatt GBL would be needed. It would take only 0.1 millisecond for the laser light to make a round-trip through the atmosphere, but it would have to be focused on the moving target for several seconds. Theoretically, adaptive optics could compensate for the effects of turbulence on the beam. *See* ground-based free-electron laser; laser; 10-kilojoule criterion.

ground-based laser uplink: *See* ground-based free-electron laser.

ground segment: The user terminals or components of space systems.

guidance: Technological control of a missile or flight pattern. Guidance systems compare a measured navigational course with a required one and then make the needed computations to correct the differences between the two. The computations yield the required velocity (translation) and altitude (rotation) corrections and changes. *See* control; navigation.

h

Hagelstein, Peter: Inventor of the X-ray laser. As a twenty-four-year-old researcher at the Lawrence Livermore National Laboratory in 1979, he developed the software that described the physical problems needed to be overcome in order to create the X-ray laser. In 1986 he resigned from full-time work at Livermore to teach at MIT but remains a consultant to the laboratory.

hard body: A missile in flight and the target of SDI infrared sensors. It might be difficult to pinpoint because of a huge advancing plume.

hardening: Any number of defensive measures used to render military targets less vulnerable to attack. A target's hardness is measured by the power needed per unit area to destroy it by a DEW. By definition, a hardened target is more difficult to destroy than a "soft" target. Applying the 10-kilojoule criterion, ICBMs would be hardened to withstand at least 15 kilojoules of energy per square (or cubic) centimeter. To deflect nuclear radiation, electron circuits and devices in computers also need to be hardened. The SDIO has fabricated and tested radiation-hardened, large-scale integrated circuits for spacecraft.

hard kill: The confirmed destruction of a target.

hardness: *See* hardening.

hardware: Although the hardware requirements of SDI far exceed the present state of the art, technology continues to evolve. The technology already exists to transmit data among system components at the high rates of speed needed by a BMD system. Hardware is required for the following SDI functions, excluding the weapons themselves: acquisition and tracking, target discrimination and classification, resource allocation, and surveillance.

heat capacity: A measure of the energy required to raise the temperature of any material by 1 degree. Expressed in joules/kilogram (in degrees Kelvin).

heat of fusion: The amount of energy required to convert a given amount of material from a solid to a liquid. Expressed in joules/gram.

heavy-lift launch vehicle (HLLV): A proposed space transportation system capable of lifting payloads of 100,000 to 150,000 pounds into space. In 1987 the SDIO requested supplemental appropriations of $110 million for the HLLV, and proposed that $434 million be spent on space transportation. In reorienting SDI programs to emphasize space transportation, the SDIO appears to be emphasizing a near-term deployment of space-based kinetic-kill vehicles. The Air Force Systems Command wants an HLLV that lifts material into space for about $1,000 per pound by 1992 and $200 to $400 per pound by the year 2000. This would represent an extensive reduction in operating costs experienced at present by NASA and the Department of Defense. *See* space transportation.

HEDI: *See* high-endoatmospheric defense interceptor.

HELSTF: *See* high-energy laser systems test facility.

hen house: Nickname for the Soviet early-warning radar that is part of its Galosh ABM system around Moscow. The U.S. Department of Defense reports that there are eleven other such radars at six sites along the Soviet border. The Soviets are said to be constructing six new phased-array, early-warning radars that can track more ballistic missiles with greater accuracy than can the hen house radars. Five of them match or supplement the coverage of the hen house radars, but the sixth, under construction at Abalakova in the Krasnoyarsk region of central Siberia, 750 kilometers from Mongolia and oriented northeast, appears to violate the ABM Treaty because—unlike the others—it is not on the periphery of the country and pointing outward.

HEO: A high-earth orbit; an orbit greater than 5,600 kilometers.

Hertz Foundation: The source of fellowships to graduate science students who agree to work at the Lawrence Livermore National Laboratory. Founded by John D. Hertz (of Hertz auto rental), the foundation is strongly anti-Soviet; Edward Teller and Lowell Wood sit on its board of directors. It is based in Livermore, California.

HF: *See* hydrogen fluoride.

high-brightness relay (HIBREL) project: A major DEW experiment of SDI that aims to demonstrate the feasibility of relay mirrors for GBLs. The experiments are not fully defined; the use of mirrors aboard the space shuttle is designed to demonstrate only the capacity to handle light from low-power lasers. *See* brightness.

high-endoatmospheric defense interceptor (HEDI): One of three major SDI tests of fixed ground-based BMD components (the other two are ERIS and TIR). This one aims to demonstrate the ability of long-range interceptor missiles controlled by an airborne ladar to intercept strategic missile warheads, in a terminal phase, within and above the atmosphere. It will be done at White Sands Missile Range, New Mexico, and at Kwajalein Missile Range with fixed ground-based launchers that cannot be reloaded rapidly. Each interceptor missile will deliver only one nonnuclear warhead. These conditions make the program valid under the terms of the ABM Treaty.

Beginning in 1989 there will be five tests of the three-stage interceptor—a combination Spartan-Sprint missile. (It uses the first stage of the Spartan and the first two stages of the

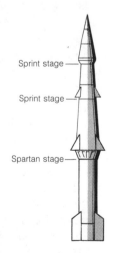

high-endoatmospheric
defense interceptor

Sprint.) McDonnell Douglas, the prime contractor, has been awarded $330 million for designing, testing, and systems engineering. Hughes Aircraft and Aerojet Company, two subcontractors, are responsible for the homing and guidance systems, and the kinetic-kill vehicle.

high-energy laser systems test facility (HELSTF): Located at White Sands Missile Range, New Mexico, this facility has the hardware to test deuterium fluoride (chemical) lasers and associated concepts of lethality and vulnerability of potential targets.

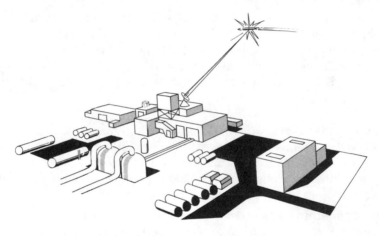

high-energy laser systems test facility

High Frontier Program: The most publicized proposal for early deployment of a BMD, presented by Lt. Gen. Daniel Graham in 1982. The study recommended the early deployment of a terminal defense of hardened targets and a space-based, boost-phase area defense—the global ballistic missile defense system—which would use rocket-powered, kinetic-kill vehicles. More effective space-based defenses would be deployed when developed. This program included a proposal for system architecture, the cost of which was estimated at $20 billion over the first five years, and $35 billion through 1990. Critical studies since have shown that the program severely underestimated costs (more realistic Pentagon estimates range from $50 to $75 billion or more) and overestimated the capabilities of the BMD system proposed. *See* deployment.

high-power radio frequency (HPRF) weapons: Devices capable of producing intense, damaging beams of radio frequency wavelength radiation—that is, electromagnetic radiation at wavelengths of 1 millimeter or more. Such devices, including microwave generators, could be designed for use in space or on the ground. The weapons would have to be large in order to concentrate great amounts of the energy into a narrow beam.

HLLV: *See* heavy-lift launch vehicle.

HOE: *See* homing overlay experiment.

homing device: A piece of equipment, mounted on an interceptor missile, that uses sensors to detect or predict the position of a target. During the flight of a missile, the device updates information constantly, guiding the missile to its target. Whether infrared homing devices can function in the upper atmosphere is not known. If they cannot, SDI interceptors will have to wait for boosters to leave the atmosphere before trying to intercept them. (Homing outside the atmosphere was demonstrated in June 1984 in the homing overlay experiment by the U.S. Army. Then, a homing detector succeeded in finding a cool target outside the atmosphere. Similar technology is used by the Air Force's air-launched ASAT weapon.)

homing overlay experiment (HOE): A ground-based U.S. ABM interceptor, permitted under the ABM Treaty. It is nonnuclear, and it may have some inherent ASAT capabilities. In June 1984 it destroyed an incoming ballistic missile outside the earth's atmosphere, demonstrating the kill capability available in a late boost or midcourse defense. The speed of the interceptor when it collided with the target was 20,000 miles per hour; the target had been launched 4,000 miles away. The concept has now been expanded further by SDIO into ERIS; Lockheed is manufacturing the new interceptor. *See* exoatmospheric reentry-vehicle interceptor subsystem.

Horning, James J.: Consulting engineer and researcher for the SDIO who has expressed reservations about the ability to develop software to support battle-management systems. Horning contends it would be too complex to meet the rigid demands of functionality, coordination, and reliability and agrees with David Parnas in calling needed SDI software unfeasible. He currently works for the Digital Equipment Corporation.

horserace acquisition studies: A series of studies sponsored by SDIO in 1984 that were to lead to expertise by U.S. industries on architectures for BMD. Ten industrial contractors were asked to define and assess alternative BMD systems, providing requirements for sensors, weapons, space power, and command, control, and communications (C3), as well as defining critical issues of implementation. In the summer of 1985 these contractors were pared down to five. Their "Systems Architecture and Tradeoff Study" reinforced the view of the critical importance of boost-phase intercept; the need for discrimination of decoys from warheads; the possibility of midcourse and terminal intercept; the basing of defensive systems in space; and the roles of C3, battle management, threat modeling, survivability, and target vulnerability. In phase two, which began in 1986, they examined the classes of architecture and defensive issues in greater detail. Contracts totaling about $8 million were awarded in January 1987. In line with this series of studies, the SDIO asked twelve teams of U.S. and European contractors in late 1986 to bid for the theater-defense architecture study focusing on the defense of Western Europe. *See* architecture; Europe.

HPRF: *See* high-power radio frequency (weapons).

Hughes Aircraft Company: A defense contractor involved in practically every aspect of SDI research and development, particularly work on the high-endoatmospheric defense interceptor (HEDI) and the space-based kinetic-kill vehicle (SBKKV). The company is headquartered in Los Angeles.

hydrogen fluoride (HF): The lasant molecule made up of hydrogen and fluorine. Since the atmospheric absorption of HF infrared radiation does not permit ground-basing of an HF chemical laser, researchers envision a space-based, 20-megawatt HF chemical laser, with a wavelength of 2.7 microns, that could conceivably direct a beam down to 10 kilometers or so above the earth. Deeper penetration would not be needed to attack ICBM boosters, since below 10 kilometers clouds would obscure the boosters. The HF laser, used in conjunction with a 10-meter mirror, would have, theoretically, a 0.32-microradian divergence angle. The spot would be 1.3 meters (4 feet) in diameter at a range of 4,000 kilometers. If dwell time were at least 7 seconds, the laser could deliver the necessary 10 kilojoules/cubic centimeter to destroy the target. *See* chemical laser.

hypercube project: An attempt, at the Jet Propulsion Laboratory, to couple many small computers together to form an extremely fast single computer.

hypersonic speed: More than five times the speed of sound.

hypervelocity weapon: A weapon that shoots projectiles and pellets at enormous speeds. One goal of SDI is to develop low-mass, high-velocity projectiles capable of intercepting fast-burn boosters in low altitude and discriminating warheads from decoys in the midcourse phase. In laboratory testing by SDI scientists, low-mass particles in dense metallic plasma have been accelerated to hypersonic speeds (40 kilometers/second). Bursts of five projectiles, fired within 0.5 seconds,

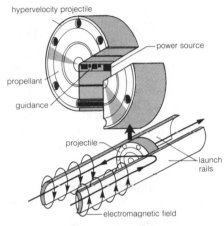

hypervelocity weapon

have been attained. According to SDI, the new power systems that store the energy for these accelerators have three times the storage-energy density of older designs. SDI officials now believe that they may have near-term applications for hypervelocity weapons to distinguish warheads from decoys. One project would involve hypervelocity pellets driven by a nuclear explosion, a sort of nuclear shotgun that would strip away decoys, thereby revealing warheads in a "threat cloud."

Some physical principles have yet to be proven, but Los Alamos scientists are encouraged by preliminary experiments conducted in this project. SDI scientists speculate that this project may have more immediate potential for midcourse discrimination than neutral particle beams. They have stepped up testing of the project and requested extra funding to verify the work.

ĭ

ICBM: *See* intercontinential ballistic missile.

imaging: A means of discrimination in which electronic and other emissions are used to develop pictures of objects and areas. Advances in this technology have been greater than anticipated. Imaging permits the transformation of light energy into electric signals and greatly reduces reaction time to minutes, or even seconds. It is an important technique for arms control verification. *See* discrimination.

imaging radar: *See* sensor, active.

impulse: A mechanical jolt, or a series of mechanical jolts, delivered to an object. An impulse can be a force applied for a period of time. The unit used to measure the strength of an impulse is the newton-second (n-s).

impulse intensity: Mechanical impulse per unit area. The unit of impulse intensity is the pascal-second (pa-s).

impulse kill: The destruction of a target by ablative shock. Impulse kill is one of three types of kill mechanisms employed by DEWs. Impulse kill, more complex and less well understood than thermal kill, would use the intensity of directed energy to deliver a mechanical shock wave to the target. This type of kill mechanism might be effective against boosters, but it would require prodigious laser pulses and mirrors to focus it. *See* functional kill; kill mechanism; thermal kill.

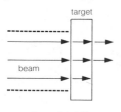

impulse kill

impulse, specific: The gauge of a rocket's performance; the time it takes 1 pound of rocket fuel to produce 1 pound of thrust. The greater the time, the hotter the rocket's engines. For the space shuttle, for instance, the specific impulse is calculated at 455 seconds. Rockets with a low specific impulse must be large enough to carry great amounts of fuel. Most Soviet rockets, for example, carry huge quantities of liquid fuel. By comparison, most U.S. rockets rely on lighter weight, more efficient solid fuel.

inclination angle: The angle of a satellite's orbit with respect to the equator. An equatorial orbit has an inclination of 0 degrees for a satellite traveling eastward and 180 degrees for one traveling westward. An orbit whose inclination is less than 90 degrees and traveling eastward is called prograde, one greater than 90 degrees is called retrograde, and at 90 degrees it is referred to as polar.

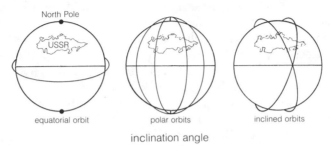

equatorial orbit   polar orbits   inclined orbits

inclination angle

inertial guidance: The steering of a ballistic missile's rocket thrust to a specified altitude where the engines will be cut off. At this point the missile flies in its ballistic missile trajectory.

inertial navigation: Calculations of a missile's position and velocity by inertial sensing. The determination of that component of a missile's motion due to gravity.

inertial sensing: A guidance technique that measures changes in a missile's motion caused by all forces except gravity. Inertial sensing uses Newton's laws to measure a missile's translation- and rotation-motion changes.

INF: *See* intermediate-range nuclear forces.

in-law test: A partly tongue-in-cheek criterion for proposed arms control. Defense analysts argue that, if a prospective arms constraint cannot be readily understood by one's in-laws, it should be simplified.

innovative science and technology (IST) program: A program within SDIO that encourages U.S. scientific and academic communities to participate in SDI research. Its director, James A. Ionson, has claimed that "virtually everyone on every campus" desires to be part of SDI. The remark sparked angry protests by the physics departments of the University of Illinois and Cornell University, among others. There, faculty members drew up petitions, labeling SDI as "deeply misguided and dangerous" and vowed neither to solicit funds nor to encourage others to participate.

The IST office sponsors research in six areas: advanced high-speed computing, materials and structures for space applications, sensing and discrimination, advanced space power, space sciences and experimentation, and directed- and kinetic-energy concepts. The research is implemented through science agents within other governmental agencies, including the Office of Naval Research, Air Force Office of Scientific Research, Army Research Office, Defense Nuclear Agency, NASA, Department of Energy, and Department of Defense laboratories. Within the last two years, the IST office has fabricated a new composite—lithium alumina silicate glass, reinforced with silicon carbide fibers—that it claims is lightweight, laser resistant, and exhibits large tensile strength, making it promising for space structures. The office also has used computer-aided design to help synthesize a polymer from resins of vinylidene fluoride and tetrafluoroethylene. The polymer will be used in the construction of supercapacitors for power storage, possibly 250 kilojoules of energy in a small container.

The IST played a part in helping to construct an optical, bistable switch as part of its effort to develop an optical supercomputer; developed an ultrahigh-energy density minicapacitor (with a 1.0-microfarad storage capacity at 5.5 volts in a container of 15 cubic centimeters) and the cryocooler, in its efforts to minimize the size of space-power sources; and continues to investigate the feasibility of the gamma-ray laser. *See* Mossbauer spectroscopy.

integrated operational nuclear detonation detection system (IONDDS): A U.S. military sensor system that detects nuclear detonations in order to monitor compliance with the Limited Test Ban Treaty.

intercept: The act of destroying a target.

interceptor missile: A space-based, boost-phase interceptor proposed in the BMD study, "Fiscal and Economic Implications of Strategic Defense," by Barry M. Blechman and Victor Utgoff. Clustered in groups of fifty in battle stations, and controlled by battle-management satellites, each interceptor, weighing 150 kilograms and carrying a 5-kilogram homing warhead, supposedly would accelerate 9 to 10 kilometers/second to intercept an ICBM booster. A potential candidate for this kind of missile is an ASAT interceptor being developed by LTV at a cost of $12 million.

intercontinental ballistic missile (ICBM): A missile with a range of 4,800 to 12,000 kilometers. The term is applied only to land-based systems in order to differentiate them from SLBMs, which, although they are considered strategic, are not necessarily intercontinental.

interim agreement: *See* SALT I and II.

intermediate-range nuclear forces (INF): The total number of nuclear-armed missiles and bombers that have a range between 1,000 and 4,800 kilometers. This range is greater than that of short- and medium-range ballistic missiles. In Europe and Asia, U.S. INFs include 40 launchers with four single-warhead, ground-launched cruise missiles; 108 Pershing IIs; and 341 Soviet SS-20 missiles.

inverse synthetic aperture radar (ISAR): A radar that uses information based on the motion of targets in order to obtain a finer resolution. *See* synthetic aperture radar.

invite, show, and tell (ISAT): U.S. and allied contractors on SDI will be asked by the SDIO to identify existing hardware for use in any proposed theater defense of Europe. Components and systems then would be tested in the national test bed.

INW: *See* isotropic nuclear weapon.

IONDDS: *See* integrated operational nuclear detonation detection system.

ionization: The removal of one or more electrons from, or the addition of one or more electrons to, a neutral atom, which then forms a charged ion. This process can limit the spreading of particle beams because the ionization of air molecules creates a conducting channel for the charged beams. When it comes to the propagation of laser beams, however, ionization, or electrical breakdown, can be a problem. The ionization of the air through which the laser beams would pass can create plasma, which then would inhibit passage of the beams. *See* particle beam.

Ionson, James A.: Director of the SDIO's program on innovative science and technology.

IR: infrared.

IRBM: intermediate-range ballistic missile.

ISAT: *See* invite, show, and tell.

isotropic: Spreading in all directions equally. When applied to radiation, it means that the radiation spreads with equal intensity everywhere. The term is used to distinguish isotropic nuclear weapons from DEWs.

isotropic nuclear weapon (INW): A nuclear explosive that radiates X-rays and other forms of radiation with equal intensity in all directions.

Israel: This nation has signed agreements with the United States to work on SDI. A $10-million contract calls for Israel to investigate a combined chemical and electrical propulsion scheme for projectiles fired by the railgun. The aim is to reduce the weight of the gun barrel and the size of the power source that would be needed to shoot electromagnetic projectiles in ground- or space-based applications. Other Israeli contractors are working on developing short-wave chemical lasers and defining theater defense architectures for Europe.

IST: innovative science and technology (program).

Italy: In agreeing to cooperate with the United States in researching SDI, contractors in Italy are investigating radar systems to acquire and track RVs outside the atmosphere, refining cryogenic coolers, and defining theater defense architectures of Europe. *See* European defense.

j

Janus: A scheduled field test by the SDIO to obtain signatures of rocket plumes at close range.

Japan: This nation, which has agreed to participate in SDI research programs, could be a low-cost supplier of BMD technology. This could include optical data storage devices, lasers and laser diodes, mercury cadmium tellurium alloys for infrared imaging, optical fiber networks, liquid crystal displays, imaging chips for graphic displays, and high-density computer memories. In addition, the SDIO is interested in Japanese expertise in parallel processing and artificial intelligence. Japanese firms expected to be involved in research include Hitachi, Fujitsu, NEC, Mitsubishi Electric, and Toshiba.

Jet Propulsion Laboratory: The research facility based at the California Institute of Technology, Pasadena, where new approaches to the use of hardware in battle management are being investigated. *See* hypercube project.

jitter: A slight wavy movement or bounce.

joule: A unit of energy; 1 kilowatt-hour equals 3.6 million joules.

k

KBSA: *See* knowledge-based software assistant.

keep-out zone: Any area of outer space that is off limits. This kind of zone may be negotiated or unilaterally declared, but the right to defend such a zone and the legality of unilaterally declaring such a zone under the Outer Space Treaty remain open to question.

Kelvin temperature: A scale in which absolute zero temperature is equated with 0 degrees Kelvin.

Keplerian orbit: A circular orbit about the center of the earth. An orbit that a satellite would follow if the earth were a uniform sphere with no atmosphere. Such an orbit would be an ellipse with the center of the earth as one focus.

KEW: *See* kinetic-energy weapon.

Keyworth, George: Former White House science adviser who has long been the GBL's most enthusiastic supporter. Keyworth has stated that the destruction of 1,000 boosters per minute is possible with SDI.

kill assessment: The determination as to whether an attempted interception had been successful. Kill assessment would be a task of any BMD-layered architecture. The destruction of targets would be noted, and information on any failures would be used in subsequent defensive attacks.

kill mechanism: The means by which SDI weapons—lasers, particle beams, and KEWs—would destroy a target. *See* functional kill; impulse kill; thermal kill.

kill time: The amount of time a weapon needs to destroy a target at a given distance. For a DEW, kill time would be proportional to the target's hardness and the square of its distance from the target, and inversely proportional to the weapon's brightness. To determine the actual kill time, slew or retarget time also would be taken into account.

kinetic-energy weapon (KEW): A weapon that collides with its target to destroy it. Today, such a weapon can only be propelled chemically and only within the atmosphere. SDI researchers are investigating the use of hypervelocity electromagnetic railguns that would be used for non-nuclear defense in boost, postboost, and midcourse phases of a missile attack.

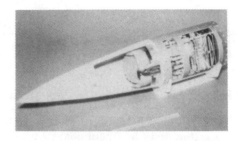

kinetic-energy weapon

SDI also is looking at the use of space-based battle stations that would house a large number of interceptor rockets or electromagnetically launched projectiles. For boost-phase interception, sensors would have to detect a launch, and then pass tracking information to a battle station. Interceptors would be assigned, aimed, and launched at the targets. Homing devices would guide the projectiles to targets. In postboost and midcourse phases, long-wave infrared detectors would be employed to discriminate between decoys and warheads. *See* homing overlay experiment; space-based kinetic-kill vehicle (project).

kinetic-energy weapons program: An SDI research effort into the design and use of KEWs for all phases of BMD, including the defense of satellites. The research builds on the U.S. Army's long-term involvement in developing BMD. The areas under study for both space- and ground-based weapons include fire control/guidance and booster propulsion, exo- and endoatmospheric interception, capabilities against shorter range threats, and the potential of electromagnetic railguns. According to the Department of Defense, all experiments are to adhere to ABM Treaty guidelines. Called proof-of-principle experiments, they are now being designed so that decisions about deployment can be made in the 1990s.

In the last two years, the SDIO has reported the success of the homing overlay experiment, the testing of elements such as divert propulsion thrusters, and research into the feasibility of multiple shots by a hypervelocity launcher and the use of high-g projectiles. In addition, SDIO's technology-base program is investigating the use of "smart" seekers to acquire targets rapidly and to provide highly accurate terminal homing, and it is researching the use of miniature rockets for boost-phase and midcourse interception. The major experiments in this research program are the SBKKV, the hypervelocity railgun, and the STM.

kj: kilojoule.

KKV: kinetic-kill vehicle. *See* space-based kinetic-kill vehicle program.

klystrons: high-energy, computer-switching devices.

KMR: *See* Kwajalein Missile Range.

knowledge-based software assistant (KBSA): SDI software that will make use of artificial intelligence techniques so that all programs will be as error-free as possible.

Krasnoyarsk: The region in central Siberia where, according to the Department of Defense, the Soviets are constructing a ballistic missile tracking and detection radar in violation of the ABM Treaty. *See* ABM Treaty; Soviet Union.

Kwajalein Missile Range (KMR): The field-test site located on Kwajalein atoll in the South Pacific. This missile range is one of two U.S. test sites—the other being White Sands Missile Range—designed for defensive system experiments that take place in an ABM mode. Kwajalein Missile Range was the testing ground for Spartan and Sprint ABM development. *See* ABM Treaty.

l

LACE/RME: *See* laser communications experiment/remote mirror experiment.

ladar: A light detection and ranging device, otherwise known as a laser radar or sensor. A ladar provides its own illumination by lighting up a target with a low-power visible or ultraviolet beam upon which the ladar's telescope is trained. The wider a ladar's field of view, the less it needs to know to locate a target. This kind of surveillance system or sensor could be introduced into an SDI architecture to pick up the trail of an ICBM booster, or it could be part of a GBL that would make use of mirrors in space.

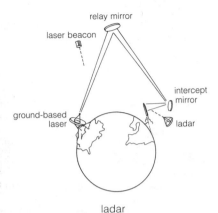

ladar

laddering down: An aggressor's hypothetical defense-suppression technique for overcoming a terminal-phase missile defense. As salvage-fused RVs attack a defense system, the detonations of one salvo disable local BMD installations so that subsequent salvos can come closer to their targets before they are intercepted. Eventually, the BMD is overcome.

LAMP: LODE advanced mirror program. *See* Alpha/LODE/LAMP.

large optics diamond turning machine (LODTM): A piece of SDI hardware that will fabricate complex mirror elements for laser battle stations. It has been built specifically to produce the cylindrically shaped mirrors for the Alpha laser.

lasant: A material that can be stimulated to produce laser light. Lasant materials can be solid, liquid, or gaseous elements or compounds. They also can take the form of plasma (ions and electrons). Actual lasants have been carbon dioxide, carbon monoxide, deuterium fluoride, hydrogen fluoride, iodine, krypton fluoride, xenon chloride, and selenium. To create laser beams out of lasants, researchers must induce a "population inversion," in which the greater proportion of lasant molecules is in an excited state. This is accomplished by using energy to "pump" lasant molecules to excited levels. Two sources of pumping energy are chemical reactions and electrical discharges. A lasant's wavelength differs according to the material used and is determined by the difference between a molecule's upper and lower states of energy.

laser: Light amplification by stimulated emission of radiation. A laser produces a narrow beam of coherent radiation. Every laser has three basic parts: an active medium, a means of excitation, and an optical cavity. The medium, or lasant, is the collection of atoms that undergoes stimulated emission. The means of excitation, or pumping, is the source of energy that causes most of the atoms in the medium to reach the state in which they emit photons. The optical cavity—usually a pair of mirrors—ensures that stimulated emission exceeds spontaneous emission, resulting in a beam of light. The laser is capable of focusing large quantities of energy at great distances.

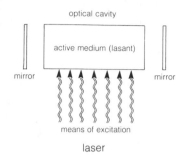

Laser light is special in two respects: its wavelength is precise, since it is produced by the same chemical transition in all the lasant molecules; and the light waves from the molecules emerge with crests and troughs aligned, since the waves are produced cooperatively. These features make it possible for mirrors to focus laser energy into narrow beams characterized by small divergence angles, or angles of spreading. But there are limits, even assuming perfect optics and perfect focusing. Generally, the smaller the wavelength, or the larger the laser mirror's diameter, the less spreading occurs and the more powerful is the beam. However, short-wavelength lasers have proven difficult to develop. Both wavelength and mirror size must be controlled to maximize the delivery of energy per unit area.

The laser is a leading candidate for boost-phase intercept of missiles in an SDI system because it could, theoretically, burn through a missile's skin (achieving what is called thermal kill), or it could cause an explosion on the target with only one short pulse (this is called impulse kill). In theory, the figures look like this: A chemical laser with a wavelength of 2.7 microns, with continuous power of 25 megawatts and a focusing mirror of 10 diameters, could burn through the skin of an ICBM booster at 3,000 kilometers if it directed 15 kilojoules of energy/square (or cubic) centimeter for 3.5 seconds. Lasers that use an optical cavity are sometimes called cavity lasers. *See* ground-based laser; space-based laser.

laser-basing: In SDI architectures, lasers could be located in space, on mountain tops, or on land for direct ascent (pop-up) into space in time of war. The space-based approach would require many laser stations (each weighing perhaps 10 tons) in geosynchronous orbit above the Soviet Union, or in lower orbits (60 degrees to the equator) circling the earth every few hours and within view of the North Pole 15 percent of the time; they would make use of battle mirrors. The GBL would use space-based relay mirrors and battle mirrors to reflect laser beams toward the ICBM boosters, but a means would have to be found to propagate the laser beam through the earth's atmosphere without losing the high quality of the beam. The pop-up technique, the most complex, would require extremely fast lift-off to send the lasers into space and then to fire at the ascending ICBM boosters. (A modified SDI architecture envisions basing lasers in Europe and making use of pop-up boosters upon a warning of an ICBM attack, but this would require European cooperation.)

laser beacon: A low-power laser that would be positioned near space-based relay mirrors in a GBL architecture. It would help overcome atmospheric distortions that would otherwise affect any laser beam aimed from the ground toward the relay mirror. The beam from the ground would be predistorted in just such a way that its passage through the same column of air as used by the laser beacon would reform it into an undistorted beam. The SDIO demonstrated the effects of atmospheric compensation in a series of experiments in 1985, which involved the propagation of a low-power laser beam from a fixed ground site to an aircraft.

laser communications experiment/remote mirror experiment (LACE/RME): A dual payload that is to be launched in late 1988 aboard a Delta rocket in the Delta 183 experiment.

laser designator: A low-power laser that would be used in a midcourse defense to illuminate a target so that a KEW weapon, such as a long-range interceptor equipped with a tracker, would be able to find it.

laser, explosive pumped: This type of laser is said to be under study in the Soviet Union. It might possibly be quite compact, with each bomb generating a single huge pulse for impulse kill of boosters. It is not clear if this would involve nuclear explosions.

laser imaging: The use of a laser to produce high-quality pictures, or images, of objects. Radar beams can be used for similar purposes. *See* laser tracker.

laser integrated space experiment (LISE): A proposed space-based test of chemical laser technology in 1990.

laser, superradiant: A laser beam that passes through the lasant only once; mirrors are not required. Free-electron lasers may be of this type. Theoretically, the laser beam would pass through an electric or magnetic field (instead of a lasant) in the presence of an electron beam.

laser tracker: A laser that would be used in a terminal-phase defense to illuminate targets so that specialized sensors could detect the reflected light and track it. It could provide imaging to determine whether targets had been destroyed and precision tracking of objects as they traveled in the midcourse phase.

lasing: The condition in which more of the lasant's molecules are in an excited high-energy state, and fewer in a low-energy state, than is usually the case. One molecule's emission sparks a chain reaction by the other molecules. Eventually, they all drop back to their original energy level, emitting radiation characterized by the same wavelength. The spreading of this process through the lasant produces a laser beam. Mirrors are usually placed at each end of the resonant cavity containing the lasant, thereby reflecting the radiation back and forth to stimulate further emission along a very narrow range of angles.

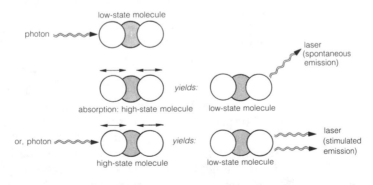

lasing

launcher: A launcher, as defined by SALT II, can be a fixed underground missile silo, a transporter-launcher for a mobile missile, a launching tube on a nuclear submarine, or a bomber that can launch a cruise missile.

Lawrence Livermore National Laboratory (LLNL): An SDI research and design facility, in Livermore, California, where the development of the X-ray laser is a major project. Laboratory scientists first successfully tested the X-ray laser at the Nevada Test Site in November 1980. The wavelength was said to have been 14 angstroms, but critics charged that the detection equipment was too unreliable to verify whether lasing had in fact occurred. Within the last two years, Lawrence Livermore Laboratory has demonstrated that charged particle beams can be guided by a laser-created channel in a low-pressure environment such as the earth's upper atmosphere. This was once considered impossible because of the earth's magnetic field. Electron beams were propagated for 60 meters in the laboratory's advanced test accelerator (ATA) and for 30 meters outside the accelerator. The success of this experiment has led to optimism about the production of charged particle beams at altitudes of 85 to 600 kilometers. In the early 1980s the laboratory also began using its ATA for experiments on induction-type free-electron lasers. To develop a 1-micron wavelength free-electron laser that SDI researchers are seeking, the ATA would have to provide 300 MeV of energy; at present it is still far from that level.

The laboratory was founded in 1952 and today employs 8,000 people. Its budget is nearly $1 billion per year. It is run by the University of California for the Department of Energy, which is responsible for ensuring civilian control. *See* ground-based free-electron laser; particle beam.

layered defense: A multileveled defense by several kinds of weapons, each corresponding to a specific phase or phases of attacking ballistic missiles. In an SDI architecture, each sequential defense layer would be independent of the others and would make use of a distinctive set of missile defense technologies. In theory, a layered defense would have a period of perhaps 30 minutes to trigger the release of its various weapons systems against incoming warheads, each layer reducing the number of enemy warheads remaining for later layers. An incoming missile would first be attacked in the boost phase, when the ICBM's booster motor is burning. Further attacks would be readied, if needed, for the postboost phase after the booster has dropped away. The next chance would come in the midcourse phase—the 20 minutes or so when the RVs and decoys coast toward their targets. Finally, if need be, the missiles' terminal or reentry phase would offer the defense one more minute or so to attack targets after the RVs reenter the atmosphere.

Each defense layer would involve the tasks of surveillance and acquisition, discrimination, target destruction, and kill assessment. All of these tasks would require fast and extensive processing of data, a concept central to a layered defense. Within seconds after launch of an attack, SDI's sensors would have to start collecting and interpreting signals or radiation emitted by, or reflected from, each of the enemy's targets. Later, exoatmospheric discrimination would be essential for midcourse defenses, which could reduce the effectiveness of fast-burn boosters.

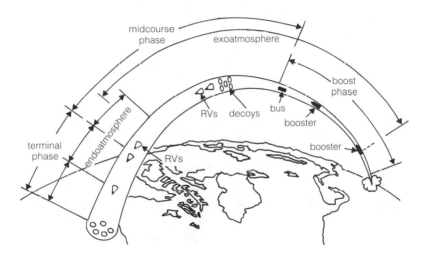

layered defense

lay-up: A process for fabricating composite structures involving the placement of sequential layers of matrix-impregnated fibers on a molded surface. *See* composite.

leakage rate: The probability that any given RV gets through an SDI system.

LEAP: *See* lightweight exoatmospheric advanced projectiles.

LEDI: *See* low-endoatmospheric defense interceptor.

Layered Defense
(From Simple to Most Complex Layer)

Layer	Description
1. **Terminal**: defense of hardened sites with rockets to intercept RVs; makes use of early-warning satellites, radar, airborne optical sensors, BM computers, and fast endoatmospheric interceptors (HEDI)	Satellites warn of launch; RVs tracked by radars and sensors; computers assign interceptors; air effects used to discriminate between RVs and decoys; SDI could be nuclear (X-ray laser)
2. **Light Midcourse**: exoatmospheric homing interceptors (ERIS), with range of hundreds of kilometers; pop-up IR sensors (or satellite-based)	RV interception above atmosphere; passive IR sensors for discrimination and kill assessment
3. **Heavier Midcourse**: ladar imaging on satellites; space-based battle management; KEW weapons; space power	Discrimination with ladars; RVs attacked with SBKKVs; good to less than 1 meter
4. **Boost Phase**: ground-based excimer or FEL; space-based mirrors for relay and aiming; high-resolution tracking and imaging; self-defense	Sensing by IR sensors; imaging by UV ladars; very bright lasers that can be used in postboost layer (lasting only 10 seconds); requires very capable BM system and kill assessments
5. **Boost Phase**: making use of an NPB for discrimination, space-based chemical lasers, and newer technologies	More interceptors are added to midcourse and terminal layers; electromagnetic railguns used for boost and postboost interceptions; great space power; highly effective software

lethality: The effectiveness of a weapon or a kill mechanism against a target. Lethality measures a weapon's ability to disable a target rather than necessarily destroy it completely.

lethality and target hardening (LTH) project: An effort within the SLKT program to assess the vulnerability of offensive weapons to SDI. The project involves investigating countermeasures to BMD, the kill mechanisms of targets, and hardening approaches. It already has measured the effect of X-rays on high-energy laser mirrors, the construction of a low-power microwave generator to study the physics of microwave weapons; and the testing of a KEW traveling at 7 kilometers/second. One of the more dramatic tests has involved the destruction of a rocket by a GBL; another has shown that small, lightweight plastic projectiles flying at 7 kilometers/second can destroy heavier aluminum targets.

leverage: The theoretical advantage gained by boost-phase intercept when destruction of the booster prevents deployment of many RVs and decoys. This action tips the cost-exchange ratio in favor of the defense and reduces the need for successful operations by follow-up layers of the defensive system. The leverage gained in the boost-phase destruction of the boosters also lessens the need to target less vulnerable RVs.

lidar: light detection and ranging. *See* ladar.

light: An electromagnetic wave that also can be considered a stream of tiny particles. Despite the fact that the waves are continuous and the particles discrete, the waves behave to some extent like particles. This wave-particle duality is a key concept in the understanding of light. *See* laser.

light amplification: The phenomenon described when the rate of stimulated energy emission exceeds the rate of absorption. *See* laser.

lightweight exoatmospheric advanced projectiles (LEAP): A research project within the SDIO's KEW program that involves the development of miniature projectiles for ground- or space-based use. The SDIO hopes to test and build lightweight projectiles by 1989.

Limited Test Ban Treaty: The treaty signed by the United States, the Soviet Union, and Great Britain in 1963, prohibiting the testing of nuclear weapons in the atmosphere, underwater, and in outer space. It permits nuclear testing underground.

linac: *See* accelerator, linear.

LISE: *See* laser integrated space experiment.

Lockheed Missile and Space Company: The defense contractor working on the space surveillance and tracking system (SSTS) and the exoatmospheric reentry-vehicle interceptor subsystem (ERIS). Lockheed is planning to conduct tests of an ERIS functional test vehicle by 1993 at a cost of $794 million. The technology that will be stressed will be the seeker, propulsion, and ordnance systems. The company is headquartered in Sunnyvale, California. *See* functional test vehicle.

LODE: large optics demonstration experiment. *See* Alpha/LODE/ LAMP.

LODTM: *See* large optics diamond turning machine.

logistics: *See* space logistics.

long-wavelength infrared (LWIR) probe: A proposed SDI research program that was to have tested fixed ground-based BMD components to assess the ability of optical system sensors to replace ABM radars. The program, which also would have examined laser components in a pop-up mode, was not funded in 1986.

Los Alamos National Laboratory (LANL): The New Mexico research and design facility for SDI weapons. One of two federal laboratories, along with Lawrence Livermore, where nuclear weapons are designed. The LANL is developing the free-electron laser for the boost-phase interception of targets and neutral particle beams for postboost-phase or terminal-phase intercept. It also has tested the second stage of a neutral particle beam device called a radio frequency quadrupole accelerator. (It has produced a 100-milliampere beam.) The Department of Energy is responsible for all production of weapons, thereby assuring civilian control.

low-endoatmospheric defense interceptor (LEDI): A short-range missile designed to intercept RVs that elude HEDI missiles in the terminal phase of an SDI system. *See* interceptor missile.

LTH: *See* lethality and target hardening (project).

LTV Corporation: The prime contractor of the U.S. Air Force's ASAT prototype weapon. Comprised of a rocket fired from an F-15 fighter plane, the weapon has been tested five times in recent years, including a 1985 experiment in which it destroyed a satellite.

LWIR: long-wavelength infrared (radiation). *See* electromagnetic radiation; long-wavelength infrared (probe).

m

McCarthy, John: Developer of LISP, a computer programming language used in artificial intelligence. A professor of computer science at Stanford University, McCarthy argues that it is possible to develop software for SDI.

McNamara, Robert: U.S. secretary of defense under President Lyndon B. Johnson who approved development of the Sentinel (later Safeguard) ABM system. Since leaving the World Bank, which he headed for many years, McNamara has spoken out against the development and deployment of SDI. He is the author of *Blundering into Disaster: Surviving the First Century of the Nuclear Age* (1986).

Madley, J. M.: Developer of the free-electron laser. Madley is now a physicist at Stanford University.

materials and structures: A research area within the SLKT program that seeks to identify and develop materials for large space structures, to be made up of lightweight platforms. These structures have not yet been tested, let alone built, for space use. Lightweight structures are now seen as essential to SDI, especially since a great amount of material will have to be launched into space to construct a complete defensive system. Within the last two years, the SDIO has begun to look at the requirements for this program, but it lags far behind other research efforts.

matrix: The composite constituent that binds and transmits loads between fibers. The primary matrix material in SDI applications is expected to be epoxies. Other matrices can be high-temperature thermoplastics that soften when heated and harden when cooled. The main materials that will be used to reinforce bindings will be carbon/graphite, aramid (a lightweight fiber), and high-strength glass fibers. *See* composite.

Maxwell Laboratories: A defense contractor located in San Diego that is developing a space-based electromagnetic railgun engineered to fire hundreds of projectiles every minute at a speed of 2 miles per second. The railgun in development is named CHECMATE— compact high-energy capacitor module advanced technology experiment— and is the size of a small airplane. *See* electromagnetic railgun.

Maxwell Laboratories: CHECMATE railgun

megawatt: A unit of power equal to 1 million watts. A typical commercial electric plant generates about 500 to 1,000 megawatts. *See* space power.

metal-matrix composites: Materials that can be used to fabricate the large relay and intercept mirrors for the proposed space-based laser systems. They offer uniformity in design, are lightweight, and have easier machinability than do conventional materials.

MeV: A unit of energy that expresses the power in nuclear processes. It stands for 1 million electron volts and is equivalent to the energy that an electron gains in crossing a potential of 1 million volts.

Meyers, Stephen: Consultant to the Defense Advanced Research Projects Agency. A professor at MIT, Meyers is an expert on Soviet BMD systems.

micron: One millionth of 1 meter; twice the wavelength of visible light.

microwave: A short-wavelength radio wave used in radar, satellite communications, and terrestrial communications relays. *See* electromagnetic radiation.

microwave generator: A theoretical DEW that would beam microwaves. The principle technical problem with a microwave-based DEW is its lethality. Since its divergence angle would be large, it would deposit a spot several kilometers wide at a range of only a few hundred kilometers. The pulse might not be intense enough to inflict damage. The technology of actually constructing the weapon is another barrier for SDI researchers. However, assuming it could be created, its application might proceed as follows: As enemy ICBMs lift off, a few space-based microwave generators attack the boosters. Their pulses act as would the high-frequency component of the electromagnetic pulse from a nuclear explosion. The weapon, in effect, would be an EMP bomb. The boosters' skins would probably prevent the EMP from reaching any internal circuitry, but other openings or conduits might not. Therefore, it is possible that their circuitry would be damaged anyway.

midcourse phase: The phase of a ballistic missile's flight during which the RVs and decoys are above the atmosphere. It is during this phase that a multilayered SDI system would first have to discriminate warheads from decoys and then try to destroy the warheads. The defense might have 20 minutes, but then again it might have even less time if it were facing SLBM RVs. In this phase an SDI system would have more time than would other defense layers to find and engage targets.

The system also would have more to do. Its major task would be to discriminate targets from decoys and debris. To identify ten RVs carried by one SS-18 postboost vehicle (PBV) in midcourse flight, the defense would have to sort through possibly hundreds of potential targets. In a massive launch, or an attempted saturation of a terminal defense, there might be thousands of targets and decoys. Leverage would be low, but the defense could be selective because the destinations of the individual RVs can be determined once they have separated from the PBVs.

A midcourse defense almost certainly will be difficult, if not impossible. To critics of SDI it sounds impractical and not very credible. SDI researchers envision a midcourse defense that uses a space-based neutral particle beam or a laser to irradiate all potential targets in flight. Any actual RVs would emit gamma rays, which would be sensed by SDI systems, but decoys would emit no radiation. The velocities of the decoys would change slightly. Actual interception of targets would make use of exoatmospheric interceptors and DEWs. Midcourse defense also could complement a terminal defense of large territories. *See* ballistic missile defense; layered defense; SDI.

Midgetman: The new U.S. ICBM that may be kept "light," at 37,000 pounds, and mobile. At first it may be designed to carry only one warhead, along with several penetration aids; later it might be upgraded to carry two warheads and no decoys. Its expected deployment in the 1990s is in response to the Soviet Union's deployment of seventy SS-25 missiles, which the Reagan administration indicated was a violation of SALT II.

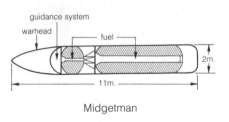

Midgetman

military satellite (MILSAT): A satellite used for navigational or intelligence gathering purposes that does meteorological surveillance and scanning of ballistic missile launch areas. It is part of the U.S. early-warning system, performing optical and radar reconnaissance of foreign forces on land and sea, interception of radio communications and radar signals, and providing logistical support of space systems in need of maintenance and retrieval of equipment.

miniature homing vehicle (MHV): An air-launched, pop-up kinetic-energy ASAT weapon being developed and tested by the U.S. Air Force. It also is called the miniature vehicle.

miniature homing vehicle

MIRACL: The mid-infra red advanced chemical laser is the largest and brightest continuous-wave laser in the West. Built by TRW for the U.S. Navy's ship defense system, MIRACL was tested in a boost-phase mode at HELSTF in July 1985. At a range of 10 to 20 kilometers, the laser's 2.2-megawatt beam reached its experimental limit. It showed promise of being able to focus onto a small spot at longer ranges, and possibly propagating through the atmosphere. Its wavelength is 3.8 microns, but it still falls short of the 1-micron wavelength desired by SDI scientists. This laser will be combined with the sea lite beam director subsystem (from the Navy's Sea Lite Program) into an experimental device for a major test in the DEW program. At White Sands Missile Range, experiments will be performed against ground-based static targets so as not to violate terms of the ABM Treaty, according to the Department of Defense. *See* chemical laser.

mirrors: The use of relay and intercept mirrors with lasers is a newer concept in strategic defense. Based in space, the mirrors would relay radiation from space- or ground-based lasers to their targets. The development of mirrors has been described by one expert as a "horrendous problem." The shorter the wavelength of the laser, the smaller the mirrors would have to be. Chemical lasers would have to have lightweight mirrors tens of meters across and divided into thousands of individually adjustable segments. Ground-based free-electron and excimer lasers would need more finely machined mirrors to tolerate smaller vibrations and stresses due to heating from their laser beams. The SDIO has announced the manufacture of a flat mirror that is less than 10 percent of the density of the space telescope's primary mirror, making it suitable for a relay mirror. In space, the mirrors could be covered by protective shields; they also could be "hidden" by various means, with the shields in place most of the time. Relay and intercept mirrors would obviate the need for many laser satellites in a BMD, helping to lessen the amount of material that would have to be launched into space for any SDI architecture.

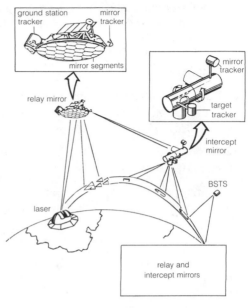

mirrors

mirrors, intercept: Small space mirrors—perhaps 5 meters across— placed in low-earth orbit as part of any space- or ground-based SDI laser architecture. The mirrors would receive the beams of light coming from relay mirrors or directly from a space-based laser, and focus the beams toward ICBM boosters for boost-phase interception. They would make use of target data supplied by ladars. The mirrors also are called battle mirrors or mission mirrors.

mirrors, relay: Large space mirrors—perhaps 30 meters across—that would be placed in geosynchronous orbits to carry beams of light from a ground-based SDI laser around the curve of the earth and then send them toward the low-earth orbit intercept, or battle, mirrors.

mirrors, rubber: Envisioned by SDI scientists as space-based relay mirrors for a GBL system, these highly sophisticated computerized mirrors would make use of honeycombed panels to direct beams of light. The panels would be adjusted to make up for the distortions that affect lasers in the earth's atmosphere.

MIRV: A multiple independently targetable reentry vehicle, packed atop a single ballistic missile. RVs on the same postboost phase can be independently placed on a ballistic course toward targets, after the completion of the boost phase.

MKV: *See* multiple-kill vehicle.

MMW: *See* multimegawatt (reactor).

"Molniya" orbits: The extreme elliptical orbits of Soviet early-warning and communications satellites and their ASAT weapons. These orbits bring the satellites close to the Southern Hemisphere.

monostatic radar: A radar system in which both the receiver and the transmitter are collocated.

Mössbauer spectroscopy: Research in spectroscopy in an effort to develop a gamma-ray laser that does not depend on a nuclear explosion as the source of its energy. It seems that it might be possible instead to make use of an external laser as the pumping source.

multimegawatt (MMW) reactor: A still theoretical source of space power for SDI, being funded by the SDIO and the Department of Energy, and explored by SDI's space nuclear power consortium. Since SDI components will need power on a large scale, the SDIO in 1985 began to investigate nuclear and nonnuclear sources of power. The MMW looks to be a pulsed, gaseous fuel reactor that can send gas through the system to provide burst-mode power for weapons systems and other components.

multiple-kill vehicle (MKV): A kinetic-energy weapon that would destroy more than one target at a time. This type of weapon is being investigated by SDI's KEW program.

multiple phenomenology: The repeated observations of potential targets by means of different physical principles and sensors.

multispectral sensing: A discriminating technique that would make use of the many visible and infrared light bands of the electromagnetic spectrum to sense a target. It would make sensing easier and deceptive measures and countermeasures more difficult to achieve. *See* sensor.

multistatic radar: A radar system with a transmitter and several receivers that are all separated.

mutual strategic security: A defensive posture in which the United States unilaterally limits its warheads to less than would be required for a first strike against the Soviet Union. At the same time, the United States would develop the two-level, near-term SDI system proposed by the George C. Marshall Institute in December 1986: space-based kinetic-kill vehicles and terminal defense interceptor missiles. Mutual strategic security was advocated by Zbigniew Brzezinski in early 1987 in the hope that it will force the Soviet Union to make concessions in arms control, or lead to a transition by both sides to use defensive systems.

MV: miniature vehicle. *See* miniature homing vehicle.

MWIR: medium-wave infrared. *See* electromagnetic radiation.

MX: The "experimental missile," the latest addition to the U.S. ICBM arsenal, permitted under the provisions of SALT II. Also called the Peacekeeper, it will contain ten warheads. At the end of 1986 the United States began deploying fifty MX missiles in silos now used by the three-warhead Minuteman III missiles. The missile, which uses solid fuel, has a fast-burn boost phase lasting about 170 seconds. Just as important, the missile has the capability to be a space-launch vehicle that could carry 5,500 pounds into a near-earth, 30-degree inclination orbit. Were it supplied with an appropriate upper stage, it could place perhaps 3,000 pounds into polar orbit.

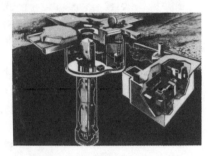

MX missile

N

National Campaign to Save the ABM Treaty: An organization that opposes SDI, headquartered in Washington, DC. The executive director is David Riley.

national command authorities (NCA): Areas and centers of military responsibility during times of crises.

national technical means (of verification): The euphemistic phrase first used in the 1972 SALT I Treaty that stands for photoreconnaissance satellites, the existence of which at the time was highly classified. Other devices nations now use to ensure that others comply with arms control agreements include radars based on land, sea, and air.

national test bed (NTB): A highly sophisticated computer system and video operation that simulates SDI. It is expected to help resolve the dilemma of whether to proceed with SDI. By 1990 it will be run at the national test facility (NTF) in combination with tests done at the national laboratories, missile ranges, and other sites. The NTB may cost $100 million to run tests of algorithms and displays of the latest space- and ground-based weapons, pop-up modes of defense, and allied antitactical ballistic missiles. It will support battle-management/C3 experiments and tests from minor to major demonstrations, and incorporate networks, processors, software, and man-machine interfaces. Realistic uses of weapons and sensors will be considered by the SDIO as well. *See* testing.

national test facility (NTF): The U.S. site where the NTB will be run. Within the Consolidated Space Operations Center at Falcon Air Force Base, Colorado Springs, the NTF will support the integration and control of all systems and experiments of SDI. Integration will test hardware operations of actual equipment such as signal processors, communications controllers, message generators, and real interfaces with other SDI systems. It also will test non-SDI national and allied assets. The first test will be a seven-part SATKA experiment in late 1987.

navigation: The determination of the position, velocity, and altitude of a vehicle. Navigational measurements include optical sightings, phase shifts and time delays of radio waves, and the reactions of inertial sensors to motion.

NAVSTAR: The U.S. military satellite that carries the IONDDS sensor for the detection of nuclear detonations. It is employed in critical missions in military satellite operations.

NCA: *See* national command authorities.

NDEW: *See* nuclear directed-energy weapon.

net defense capability: SDI's theoretical capabilities. The defense system's effectiveness will depend upon the opponent's offensive capacity, the components of the defense, and the mode of operation of the defense, for instance, passive or active. Five levels of net defense capability can be identified for an offense-dominated, transition, or defense-dominated region or territory.

System Capability	Level	SDI Description
Offense dominant	A	No defense at all
"	B	Survival of some ICBMs
Transition	C	Survival of most ICBMs, or most cities, but not both
Defense dominant	D	Survival of military targets, some cities
"	E	Urban survival against heavy attack

network concepts: A software task concerned with the specification, design, development, and validation of battle-management computer systems. The testing of SDI will involve the evaluation of the design of the computer systems. Simulations of the systems will test the operating system software and the algorithms. A further step in the process will mean the demonstration of computer systems in real-time. *See* national test bed.

neutral particle beam (NPB): An energized beam of atoms having no net electrical charge. To produce a neutral beam, powerful particle accelerators (similar to those used for scientific research, isotope production, and fusion-power applications) accelerate negative atoms—that is, atoms with an extra electron). Two kinds of negative ions often used are hydrogen and tritium. An NPB weapon within an SDI architecture might consist of a particle accelerator, beam focusing and pointing magnets, and a "stripping" device (such as a gas cell) that removes the extra electrons as the beam emerges from the accelerator at nearly the speed of light.

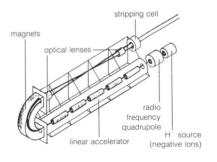

neutral particle beam

Power sources and other equipment also would be needed. An NPB might be useful in outer space as a boost-phase intercept weapon, or as a device that discriminates warheads from decoys in a midcourse defense. It would have to be about 100 feet long. Its promise is thrown into doubt by two considerations: the beam cannot propagate stably even through the thinnest atmosphere (the atoms would become ionized and hence charged), and its lethality is uncertain. As a boost-phase weapon, it would have to wait for attacking boosters to reach a very high altitude. An NPB would require a great deal of current and high energy; a "modest" figure is 800 MeV.

In space, it would require multimegawatt power sources and accelerators of great size and weight. According to some sources, an NPB spacecraft weapon with sufficient fuel to operate for 1,000 seconds would have to weigh 4 tons per megawatt of beam power. A turboalternator-powered NPB weapon might require about 25 tons of liquid hydrogen, liquid oxygen, tanks, and other equipment to deliver a dose of 10 kilograys through shielding at a range of 40,000 kilometers, thereby damaging most high-density, silicon-integrated circuits. Its beam would diverge at small angles, having a relatively small diameter even at great distances: 40 meters wide at a range of 40,000 kilometers. At present, however, it appears it will be difficult to determine whether an NPB even reaches and disables its targets. In the 1990s, SDIO plans to launch a $700-million NPB spacecraft. *See* gray; particle beam; space-based neutral particle beam.

	NPB Penetration Capability (centimeters)			
	Hydrogen		Tritium	
	100 MeV	*250 MeV*	*100 MeV*	*250 MeV*
Solid fuel	9.5	47	4	20
Aluminum	3.5	17	2	8
Lead	1	4	0.5	2

neutral particle beam (NPB) integration: A major SDI experiment that will investigate the possibilities of using an NPB in midcourse discrimination. This experiment will be conducted in outer space at low power, using nearby coorbital instrumented targets. The device will not be able to acquire or track ballistic missiles autonomously. This condition implies adherence to the terms of the ABM Treaty, according to the SDIO.

Nevada Test Site: The nuclear testing facility operated by the Department of Energy. The site comprises 1,350 acres and has been used for about twenty underground tests per year since 1963 when the Limited Test Ban Treaty was signed.

node: A way to accomplish a task. To ensure continued functioning of SDI sensors, computer systems will have to solve problems by taking different approaches, or nodes. SDI's testing of an advanced signal processor has been demonstrated in a multinodal operation, including recovery of the system after the failure of one of the nodes.

Nevada Test Site

Nova laser: One of the world's most powerful lasers. Developed by the Lawrence Livermore National Laboratory after an eight-year effort in 1985, it is testing short-wavelength beams, especially the X-ray. Its development was financed by the Department of Energy.

NPB: *See* neutral particle beam.

NTB: *See* national test bed.

NTF: *See* national test facility.

NTM: *See* national technical means (of verification).

nuclear directed-energy weapon (NDEW): A DEW that would have a specially designated nuclear explosive as its source of energy. It most likely would be an X-ray laser, a gamma-ray laser, or an EMP weapon.

Nuclear Non-Proliferation Treaty: An international agreement actually titled the "Treaty on the Non-Proliferation of Nuclear Weapons." It entered into force on March 5, 1970, and now has about 120 signatories. States that have signed this treaty take their obligations seriously. If they saw the ABM Treaty abandoned, then their adherence to nonproliferation might come into question.

	Nuclear Tests, 1945–85	
	United States	Soviet Union
1945–50	8	1
1951–55	61	18
1956–60	127	71
1961–65	207	109
1966–70	170	72
1971–75	71	91
1976–80	72	128
1981–85	83	124
Totals	799	604

nuclear weaponry: The force levels and structures of weapons among the parties to an arms control agreement.

Oak Ridge National Laboratory: A Department of Energy laboratory, based in Tennessee, that has produced ion-beam currents exceeding 100 milliamperes and lasting 5 seconds. This is important because high-brightness ion sources represent the first stage in the development of a neutral particle beam. *See* particle beam.

obscurant: Anything like smoke or chaff that would conceal an object from a radio or optical sensor.

offense-dominated strategy: The strategic posture that emphasizes offensive and retaliatory capabilities. This posture makes use of little or no defense while trying to assure the survival of retaliatory forces. As the United States moves ahead with SDI, the Soviet Union continues to see SDI as a cover to strengthen America's offensive-dominated capabilities. *See* net defense capability.

Office of Technology Assessment (OTA): The analytical arm of Congress, which in 1984 and 1985 issued reports on BMD entitled "Directed-Energy Missile Defense in Space," "Ballistic Missile Defense Technologies," and "Anti-Satellite Weapons, Countermeasures, and Arms Control."

on-line: Operating at the moment, as opposed to dormant or off-line.

opportunity costs: Money that would have been appropriated for other programs except for the fact that SDI is being developed.

optical cavity: The volume bounded by two mirrors used in the creation of a laser.

optical processing: A hypothetical type of analog processing in which light beams, instead of electronic signals, would be used for high-speed calculations.

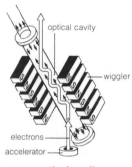

optical radiation: Electromagnetic radiation at wavelengths shorter than 1 millimeter. This kind of radiation could be produced by high-energy laser weapons by means of stimulated emission.

optical sensor: A surveillance system that detects radiation in the range of optical wavelengths. *See* sensor.

optical sighting: A navigational measurement that specifies the angle between the line of sight of an optical instrument and another line of direction into space. This angle can help establish position and altitude.

optical switch: Data transmission and switching that is handled by light rather than by electrons. In considering the need for high-speed data processing, SDI researchers contend that optical switches could permit enormous increases in computational capabilities, almost at the speed of light. Such switches could be composed of gallium arsenide or polydiacetylene, a new plastic.

optical wavelengths: Infrared, visible, and ultraviolet wavelengths.

orbital elements: The set of parameters, such as apogee, perigee, and inclination, that specifies Keplerian orbits and the positions of satellites. Orbital elements are required to specify unambiguously the position of a satellite in such an orbit and at a particular time.

orbiting patch: A conceivable Soviet defense suppression system against SDI's space-based kinetic-kill vehicles. Instead of distributing their platforms equally in orbit, the Soviets might have all their satellites bunched together in an orbiting group in space. When this "patch" came over the Soviet Union, it would attack and overwhelm the few U.S. satellites then over the USSR, thus punching a hole through which Soviet missiles could be launched.

OTA: *See* Office of Technology Assessment.

Outer Space Treaty: The 1967 treaty signed by the United States, the Soviet Union, and other nations. It forbids the basing of nuclear and other weapons of mass destruction in space.

overwhelm: To saturate SDI by multiple and successive attacks. *See* ballistic missile defense; defense suppression; SDI.

P

PAR: phased-array radar.

parallel processing: The simultaneous use of different hardware paths in a computer to solve problems. Parallel processing reduces the time to do calculations. *See* software; systems analysis/battle management.

Parnas, David: Professor of computer science at the University of Victoria, British Columbia. Parnas has served as a consultant to SDIO on the uses of computers to support battle management. His experience leads him to doubt that battle-management software could be developed; in testimony he has said that it could not be made error-free. *See* software.

particle beam: A beam of atomic particles, such as protons, electrons, neutral atoms, and heavy ions, whose energy could conceivably be deposited within a target rather than at its surface, as is the case with lasers. Only charged particles can be accelerated to form a high-energy beam, but such a beam bends uncontrollably in the earth's magnetic field. A charged particle beam probably would be less useful than a laser as a boost-phase, space-based weapon, but preliminary experiments by SDI scientists have led to some hope that against targets in low-earth altitudes it may be possible to use a brightly charged particle beam. A laser would first have to ionize a path through rarefied near-space, and then an electron beam would be fired into this channel, with the positively charged ions providing an electrostatic restoring force that would compensate for the bending forces of the earth's magnetic field.

A still less exotic conception makes use of a neutral particle beam weapon that would not be subject to the effects of the earth's magnetic field, travels in a straight line, and is more easily directed toward a target. A neutral particle beam weapon would employ hydrogen atoms, which would contain enough energy to penetrate several centimeters into any material. Because of this penetrating power—expressed as joules/gram deposited within a target—a neutral particle beam might be difficult to overcome, but such a weapon could only work, as noted, outside the atmosphere. Within the atmosphere, it would be stripped of electrons, resulting in a beam of charged protons, and subject to bending by the earth's magnetic field. The neutral particle beam, it appears, would not be effective below 100 kilometers.

At present, the SDIO considers particle beams potentially the "brightest" of all DEWs. Brightness depends on a beam's power and on how tightly the beam can be focused. Nevertheless, there are problems associated with a particle beam, both with its kill assessment—whether damage is observable—and the tracking of the beam itself. If the beam misses, it might be hard to know where it has gone. In addition, there is the problem of overcoming hardened electronic circuitry. Circuits using gallium arsenide could be 1,000 times more resistant to particle beam radiation than are those based on silicon technology. Finally, earth-bound accelerators would be too heavy and too large to generate the required beam intensities for a particle beam weapon; the accelerators would have to be in space. The implications of this are that the charged particle beam will be more difficult to propagate over great distances than would the laser. If the particle beam is seriously considered for SDI applications, it will have to be the neutral beam, which first must begin as a charged beam, because only a charged beam can be accelerated through electromagnetic forces. *See* neutral particle beam.

| | *Particle Beam versus Laser* | |
	Particle Beam	*Laser*
Design features	Particles; accelerating magnetic field; beam techniques; injection and extraction of particles	Active medium; excitation means; optical cavity; extraction of beam
SDI types	Neutral particle beam; charged particle beam	Chemical; excimer; free electron; X-ray
Weapon fired	Photons; electrons	Photons
Atmospheric interaction	Neutralization of charge	Thermal blooming
Kill mechanism	Functional kill	Impulse; thermal kill

Pathfinder: A technology integration experiment in space tracking and pointing that is to use expendable launch vehicles.

pave paws: The name of the ballistic missile early-warning radars under construction on the periphery of the United States. The radars are oriented outward.

payload: The carrying capacity of a warhead, plus the guidance equipment and any penetration aids. With a 25-percent reduction in payload, a booster the size of the MX could be built that would burn out in less time during the boost phase. *See* booster; throw-weight.

PBV: *See* postboost vehicle.

penetration aid: A decoy or any other countermeasure device mounted on a postboost vehicle that, when released, makes it more difficult for the defense system to detect and destroy incoming RVs. *See* decoy.

penetrativity: A weapon's ability to reach a target.

phase conjugation: An approach that would help a laser compensate for the effects of atmospheric disturbances on a beam. It would permit a GBL to propagate through the atmosphere by allowing a beam of light to be transmitted down through the atmosphere to a detector, whose job it is to measure distortions to the beam caused by air turbulence and any inaccuracies in the optical system itself. Then adaptive optics would imprint equal and opposite waveforms onto the beam that is to be transmitted up through the atmosphere.

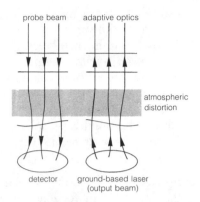

phase conjugation. A probe beam reveals atmospheric distortion. The GBL's beam is then distorted in the equal and opposite sense to cancel out any atmospheric disturbances.

phased-array radar: A radar that is made up of many smaller radars linked to yield a three-dimensional view. Its elements are physically stationary, but its beam is electronically steerable and can switch rapidly from one target to another. It is used as a component of an ABM system, to track objects at great distances, to gain early warning of an ICBM attack, and for national technical means. Large phased-array radars are needed for ASAT space surveillance and battle management.

Phoenix: A U.S. air-to-air missile.

photon: A quantum of light or a packet of light; a photon is measured in frequencies of radians/second.

photoreconnaissance satellite: A satellite that has the capability to take high-resolution photographs.

Pike, John: Associate director for space policy of the Federation of American Scientists. Pike has spoken out against SDI.

plasma: Ionized gas, sometimes referred to as the fourth state of matter. It is a component of fusion and stars and behaves much like fluid. SDI researchers are attempting to understand how plasma acts in order to develop lasers and neutral particle beams.

PLATO: *See* preliminary lethality assessment test object.

pointing and tracking: The aiming of sensors and defensive weapons at targets with sufficient accuracy for tracking and destruction. This is a task within each layer of an SDI architecture. Every target will have to be tracked before it can be destroyed. Subsequently, this tracking information would have to be sent to the appropriate defensive weapon. The tracking and pointing requirements will vary for different types of weapons. For example, kinetic-kill weapons would have to be pointed close enough for on-board sensors to acquire a target, and laser beams would have to be fixed onto a single spot on a target to inflict damage.

pointing, closed-loop: The pointing of a laser beam at a target and the receiving of feedback as to whether the pointing is accurate. The beam's divergence angle will be a critical factor in the effectiveness of the pointing.

pointing, open-loop: The pointing of a neutral particle beam at a target, with no feedback as to whether the pointing is accurate. LWIR sensors could track a target, and a ladar could help determine the appropriate angle at which to direct the beam.

polydiacetylene: A new plastic that claims to handle 1 trillion operations per second as an optical switch in computers. It is being developed by GTE Laboratories, Waltham, Massachusetts.

polymer: A substance made of giant molecules formed by the union of simple molecules called monomers.

polymer-matrix composites: Organic polymers that have been reinforced with a variety of short or continuous fibers in order to gain added strength and stiffness. One category of polymer-matrix composites is advanced composites, which are inexpensive and used primarily in the aerospace industry. *See* composite.

population inversion: The light-amplification phenomenon that occurs when the number of excited atoms exceeds the number of unexcited atoms. *See* laser.

pop-up technique: The last-minute direct ascent of a weapon into outer space. This represents a conceivable mode for basing the DEW called the X-ray laser. Following a warning of attack, SDI could pop-up its X-ray laser with specially developed submarine-launched missiles to an altitude high enough to attack one or more ICBM boosters or postboost vehicles. But the targets would have to be above a minimum engagement altitude; in this mode of basing, the weapons would not be deployed in space. Thus, the United States would not violate the Outer Space Treaty, nor face the problems associated with GBL/space-mirror schemes. A pop-up technique, however, could be overcome by fast-burn boosters.

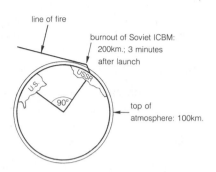

line of fire

burnout of Soviet ICBM: 200km.; 3 minutes after launch

U.S.

USSR

90°

top of atmosphere: 100km.

pop-up technique. X-ray laser would have to rise above the atmosphere, at least 100 kilometers, in order to intercept a Soviet ICBM. It would have to do this within a few minutes of the launch of the ICBM.

porcupine: A defensive satellite that might use rockets against an ASAT weapon.

porosity: In a less than perfect SDI architecture, the defense will suffer "leaks." Under a massive attack of, say, 10,000 warheads, SDI will not work. A layered defense that is 90 to 95 percent effective would still not protect population centers and territory. *See* net defense capability.

Poseidon: The U.S. sea-based missile. The total number of warheads for all Poseidons is 3,000.

postboost phase: The phase of a ballistic missile's trajectory, during which the RVs are being carried on the postboost vehicle (PBV) or bus, the container holding all the warheads when the missile is launched. It is during this phase that a multilayered SDI architecture would try to destroy the PBV or deal with the RVs individually after they are released from the PBV. Within 3 to 5 minutes after the booster rockets fall away, the RVs would be independently placed on ballistic trajectories toward their targets from the PBV. Decoys and other penetration aids also would be released by the PBV.

As the phase progressed and more RVs were released, the bus would lose value as a target. Therefore, leverage would be high only at the beginning of the phase: one direct hit of a fully loaded bus destroys several warheads. The RVs are considered to be "hard" targets and would have to be engaged early in the phase for SDI to achieve the best results. Warhead discrimination in this phase might make use of multispectral sensors of different wavelengths or a neutral particle beam. Acquisition and interception would involve the same weapons and components used for boost-phase interception. *See* ballistic missile defense; layered defense; SDI.

postboost vehicle (PBV): The bus or portion of a rocket's payload that carries the multiple warheads. A PBV can place each warhead on its final trajectory to a target.

potential constraint functions: The limitations and areas of accountability between parties to an arms control agreement.

power conditioning: The methods of converting electricity into a form usable by directed- and kinetic-energy weapons. Excimer lasers, free-electron lasers, neutral particle beams, and railguns would have to have outside sources of power and the means to convert that power for their own purposes. Chemical lasers, X-ray lasers, and rocket-propelled kinetic-energy interceptors probably would have power sources integral to the weapons themselves.

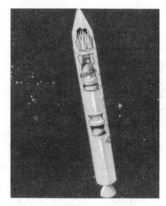

postboost vehicle

power supply: The three sources of power for space-based components being considered by SDI scientists are fuel-burning sources, explosive chemicals, and nuclear power. Ground-based systems may make use of commercial electric plants. *See* space power.

precursor burst: A countermeasure to a space-based defense that would take the form of nuclear explosions in space. This would disable sensors by creating radioactive emissions, electromagnetic pulses, and heat. *See* defense suppression.

preemptive attack: A first strike.

preemptive destruction: A first strike that aims to reduce greatly the offensive capability of an enemy.

preferential defense: *See* defense, preferential.

preferential offense: The concentration of offensive assets on a few targets.

preliminary lethality assessment test object (PLATO): The first major test at the new particle beam facility at Brookhaven National Laboratory, Long Island, New York.

prevailing: Nuclear age strategy, stressed by some conservatives, that accepts "tolerable levels of damage" commensurate with the stakes of a nuclear conflict. Effective air defenses, civil defense, and some kind of BMD would all be required in such a strategy.

processor: The part of a computer that operates on data. SDI scientists are seeking to develop algorithmically specialized fault-tolerant processors for spacecraft and aircraft. This is a task within SDI's battle-management project. It can be further broken down into the following areas of research: finding the causes of faults at the component level, looking at the development of fault-tolerant strategies in hardware and software, incorporating them into SDI architectures; discovering ways to live with faulty computer environments, and answering questions about SDI's survivability within a radiated environment. All of this and more is an attempt to come to grips with the fact that SDI's battle-management hardware and software will not be perfect but must function under battle conditions. *See* systems analysis/battle management.

proof-of-feasibility program: Major experiments by SDI scientists are intended to demonstrate the feasibility and integration of several projects. These are the integration of a high-power free-electron laser with a beam director, the design of a space-based neutral particle beam accelerator and sensor, a booster-tracking and weapons platform pointing experiment, and a study of kinetic-energy interception of an RV. *See* beam director; homing overlay experiment.

pulsed-power conditioning: Modifications in the transmission of power for the special components found in directed- and kinetic-energy weapons. This is an area of research being addressed by the SDIO's SLKT program. Pulsed-power conditioning would take the raw energy generated by prime energy sources and meet the special electrical energy requirements of, say, switches, power distribution elements, radio frequency sources, and intermediate energy stores.

pulse waveform: The wave pattern of a laser's beam. Depending on the type of beam, it is a single pulse, repetitive pulse, or continuous wave. *See* laser.

pumping: The energy that must be supplied to molecules to raise them to higher energy states so that laser beams can be created. The pumping energy for a chemical laser comes from the chemical reaction that makes the lasant molecules: hydrogen and fluoride reacting to form hydrogen fluoride molecules in an upper state. The pumping for other types of lasers may be electrical or nuclear. *See* laser.

q

quarry: A target.

r

rad: A unit of absorbed dose of ionizing radiation. One rad is equal to 0.001 gray.

radar ocean reconnaissance satellite (RORSAT): A military satellite that detects, locates, and classifies ships by picking up radar echoes. The satellite's orbit is usually at 250 to 450 kilometers.

radian: A unit of angular measure, equal to 57.3 degrees.

radiant energy: The energy from radiation such as electrons, protons, and alpha particles.

radio frequency linear (RFL): A type of design for the free-electron laser in which electrons are accelerated by microwaves. Now being studied by the Los Alamos National Laboratory, Stanford University, Boeing, and TRW in their attempts to achieve power levels needed for SDI applications, the RFL free-electron laser is said to have a wavelength of 0.5 microns in some applications and might be able to generate tens of megawatts by 1991, according to the Pentagon. *See* ground-based free-electron laser.

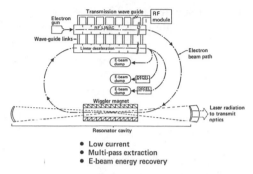

- Low current
- Multi-pass extraction
- E-beam energy recovery

radio frequency linear

radio frequency quadrupole: A highly advanced type of accelerator that speeds up and bunches a particle beam. The radio frequency quadrupole has made the development of a neutral particle beam weapon possible because it is much smaller than other kinds of accelerators. SDI scientists have fabricated and tested the preaccelerator section of a radio frequency quadrupole. They consider the accelerator—developed in the Soviet Union in the late 1960s—a major step in ion accelerator technology.

radio frequency quadrupole

radio navigation: Navigational calculations of radio signal phase shifts and time delays between a transmitter and a receiver. This provides data on range, range rate, and direction.

RADLAC: The name of the electron accelerator at Los Alamos National Laboratory. *See* Los Alamos National Laboratory.

Raman conversion: A technological process applied to excimer lasers that improves the laser's single-aperture power and beam quality. It may lead to finding a way to reduce the complexity and cost of generating high-energy excimer laser beams. A proof-of-principle test of Raman conversion has been done on the laboratory level by SDI scientists.

Raman scattering: The unwanted spreading of a laser beam when it is propagated through the atmosphere. The interaction of air molecules with the beam results in photons being emitted and energy lost. As a result, less energy is available to a laser-based DEW. The scattering increases with the laser's wavelength. In particular, Raman scattering is a problem for induction-type free-electron lasers.

reaction decoy: A decoy deployed only upon the warning or suspicion of imminent attack.

real-time protocols: Computer programs capable of reacting as soon as input is received.

redout: The blinding, or dazzling, of infrared detectors because of nuclear explosions in the upper atmosphere. High levels of infrared radiation could cause a kind of radar blackout of terminal-phase airborne optical sensors. The use of airborne optical sensors is viewed by scientists as an important supplement to the use of ground-based radars; therefore, overcoming redout is a major problem. *See* terminal phase.

red team: Researchers and scientists within the SDIO whose job it is to probe all possible countermeasures to SDI architectures.

reentry: The return of objects, launched from earth, into the atmosphere.

reentry vehicle (RV): The part of the ballistic missile containing a nuclear warhead. It is released from the last stage of a booster rocket, or from a postboost vehicle, early in the ballistic trajectory. An RV can be thermally insulated to survive the rapid heating of reentry, and it is designed to protect its contents until detonation. Critics of SDI contend that it will be difficult, and probably impractical, to intercept RVs with space-based defenses during the midcourse phase because of the problem of discriminating RVs from decoys until the decoys reenter

reentry vehicle

the atmosphere and burn up. The SDIO, however, is considering the use of a neutral particle beam weapon as an aid to discrimination. *See* midcourse phase.

repetitive pulse laser: A laser that would fire its beam in short bursts instead of as a continuous beam or a single pulse.

requirements pull: That which is viewed to be necessary. Requirements pull is one way in which technological evolution influences strategy and mandates changes to strategy.

retaliation only: The nuclear age strategy that adopts the principle of no first use of nuclear weapons. A policy of retaliation only questions whether there is any military utility attached to nuclear weapons. *See* arms control policy; transition.

retarget time: Slew time.

RFL: *See* radio frequency linear.

robust: A system's ability to endure and perform its functions well. The ability to survive under direct attack.

RORSAT: *See* radar ocean reconnaissance satellite.

Ruina, Jack: Former director of the Defense Advanced Research Projects Agency. Ruina is now a professor at MIT.

rules of the road: Restrictions nations could impose against provocative activities in space. Rules of the road could prohibit unexplained close approaches to foreign satellites and any irradiation of satellites with DEWs. With such agreed restrictions in place, any violations would justify defensive or retaliatory measures. *See* arms control policy.

RV: *See* reentry vehicle.

S

SA/BM: *See* systems analysis/battle management.

Safeguard: The U.S. midcourse and terminal-phase ABM defense of Minuteman silos, deployed in 1974 in Grand Forks, North Dakota, and deactivated one year later because of high maintenance costs. From the mid-1960s until 1969 an ABM system called Sentinel was

being designed to protect population centers. Under President
Richard M. Nixon, Sentinel was
renamed Safeguard, and the
emphasis shifted to protection of
retaliatory nuclear forces. Under
the terms of the 1972 ABM
Treaty, the United States was
permitted one ABM site with 100
ballistic missile interceptors. The
ABM system's long-range,

Safeguard ABM site, 1974

nuclear-tipped interceptor was called Spartan; the short-range interceptor was called Sprint. The battle-management early-warning radar
operated in the range of 3,600 megahertz.

SALT I and II: *See* Strategic Arms Limitation Talks.

salvage fuse: A nuclear warhead preset to detonate when attacked. A
salvage-fused warhead could serve as a countermeasure to a terminal
defense system that uses nonnuclear interceptors. The warhead could
explode as soon as the interceptor came within a certain range. *See*
terminal phase.

SAM: surface-to-air missile.

Sandia National Laboratories: An NPB research facility located in
Albuquerque, New Mexico, and run by the Department of Energy.
It has fabricated a microprocessor chip capable of absorbing a 100-
kilogray dose of gamma radiation and withstanding 140 MeV particles. Sandia also has been trying to develop a single microprocessor
chip hardened to withstand 10 kilograys, and it is the site for the
powerful fusion accelerator—the PBFA-1, or Saturn.

SAR: *See* synthetic aperture radar.

SATKA: *See* surveillance, acquisition, tracking, and kill assessment.

Saturn: The SDI name for Sandia National Laboratories' particle beam
fusion accelerator (PBFA-1). It has been used to study the design
and effects of an X-ray laser without the need for an actual X-ray
laser.

SA-X-12: A Soviet surface-to-air interceptor that has the potential to
intercept ballistic missiles. It is said to be part of a new Soviet ABM
system, which supposedly is nearing deployment stage in 1987.

SBHRG: *See* space-based hypervelocity railgun.

SBKKV: *See* space-based kinetic-kill vehicle (project).

SBL: *See* space-based laser.

SBNPB: *See* space-based neutral particle beam.

SBPB: space-based particle beam. *See* particle beam.

SCC: *See* Standing Consultative Commission (for SALT).

SDI: *See* strategic defense initiative.

SDIO: *See* Strategic Defense Initiative Organization.

sea-launched cruise missile (SLCM): Like other cruise missiles, this one flies at a very low altitude, safe even from lasers. *See* architecture.

security: Measures adopted to guarantee freedom and secrecy of action and communications. Any battle-management system would have to be secure enough to repulse attempts at penetration and subversion. However, there is still no known way to design absolute security into the functions of weapons release and ordnance safety.

selectivity: The choosing of a set of targets, either for attack or defense.

sensor: An electronic instrument that can detect radiation at great distances. Sensor detection data would be critical to such functions as acquisition, tracking, aiming, discrimination, attacking, and kill assessment. Under present SDI technology, sensors cannot detect every type of electromagnetic radiation. Various technological candidates for sensors exist, each of which would operate in a distinct

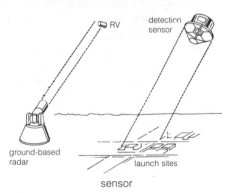

SDI layer. Detection sensors would pick up infrared radiation (short or medium wavelength) from the exhaust plumes of ICBM boosters and pass the information to pointing and tracking sensors. Postboost and midcourse sensors—having antennas 300 feet long—would pick up LWIR radiation from warheads, satellites, decoys, and debris.

These sensors also would be used in space surveillance to keep track of satellites and space mines.

The latest research indicates that neutral particle beams could be used in this defensive layer. Targets irradiated by a high-energy neutral particle beam would presumably emit gamma rays, neutrons, and other observable particles, just as they would if they were bombarded by natural cosmic rays. The gamma rays then could be detected by a gamma-ray spectrometer such as those used by U.S. lunar landers, the *Apollo* spacecraft, and the Soviet Venusian landers. In a terminal defense, ground-based radars, airborne optical detectors, and infrared detectors would spot RVs about to reenter the atmosphere. The current SDI program calls for three major experimental projects—BSTS, SSTS, and AOA—to examine sensor technology. Sensors are likely to be the most vulnerable part of a defensive satellite, subject to countermeasures by lasers, radiation, and nuclear bursts. *See* airborne optical adjunct; boost surveillance and tracking system; space surveillance and tracking system.

sensor, active: A space surveillance system composed of both a detector and a source of illumination; a sensor that would work on the same principle as radar, and that could support a GBL system or the use of kinetic-kill weapons. An active sensor would irradiate a target and detect its reflected light. At optical wavelengths—infrared, visible, and ultraviolet—this would permit kinetic-energy interceptors to keep their targets continuously in sight, thereby correcting their own courses until the end of flight. The ladar is one example of an active sensor. *See* ground-based laser.

sensor integrated discrimination experiment (SIDE): A proposed space-based test of whether sensor technology could distinguish warheads from decoys in 1990.

sensor, LWIR: A passive sensor that would be able to detect LWIR thermal radiation. Every target emits electromagnetic radiation naturally as a result of thermal processes; the amount depends on the target's surface area and temperature. Double the temperature and the radiation increases sixfold. An LWIR sensor would theoretically be able to search for objects already in space (deployed warheads, satellites, decoys, or debris) without having to observe any launchings. It could provide independent backup for SDI's launch surveillance systems. Since the earth is a powerful LWIR emitter, the

LWIR sensor would have to search looking away from the earth, either above the horizon (for low-orbiting objects), or below the horizon. The former is less complicated and is thus preferred for space-based surveillance systems. Any LWIR radiation would have to be detected by sensors cooled to near-absolute zero by cryocoolers to prevent the sensor's own radiation from being confused with that from other bodies. LWIR detection is not yet available.

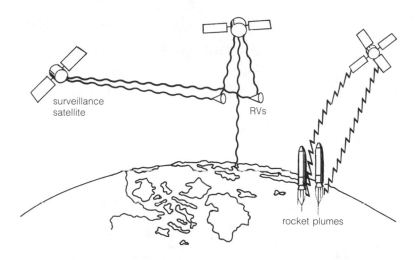

surveillance satellite

RVs

rocket plumes

sensor, LWIR. The plumes of rockets, which emit short-wave infrared radiation, can be detected against the earth's background. However, RVs emit LWIR radiation, which is difficult to pick up against similar radiation from the earth. Thus, surveillance satellites can more readily detect the presence of RVs against a space background.

sensor, passive: A space surveillance system capable only of detecting radiation naturally emitted from a target—that is, infrared radiation, or radiation that is reflected from a target. A passive sensor could be designed for long-range detection of cold bodies in space in a boost phase, the detection of simple lightweight objects in a mid-course defense, and the birth-to-death tracking of designated objects to support the use of kinetic-kill vehicles in a terminal-phase defense. In most cases, this kind of sensor would be preferred over an active sensor because it does not require the use of a high-power irradiation source. Consequently, it is itself more difficult to find by the offense. Also, its effective range could be increased more economically. Doubling its distance from a target would result in a fourfold reduction in the target radiation picked up by a passive sensor. Under the same conditions, an active sensor would pick up sixteen times less radiation. The AOA, for instance, is a passive sensor.

sensor, semiactive: A sensor that would not generate radiation but would detect it in targets when they are illuminated. Such sensors would be used for tracking and identification, and would operate without attracting attention.

Type (space-based)	Sensors Action (to target)	Phenomenon Detected
LWIR thermal imager	Pulsed laser	Thermal radiation
Multispectral imager	Pulsed laser	Reflected radiation
LWIR thermal imager	Continuous laser	Position of source of thermal radiation
Multispectral imager	Continuous laser	Reflected radiation
PB generator	Particle beams	Gamma radiation
Ionization detectors	NPB irradiation	Ionization
Gamma-ray spectrometer	NPB irradiation	Gamma radiation
Thermistor	Laser irradiation	Heating
Accelerometer	Pulsed laser irradiation	Acceleration

Sentinel: The ABM system designed in the mid-1960s that was the forerunner of Safeguard. *See* Safeguard; strategic defense initiative.

shielding: The insulation or protection of enemy targets against SDI weapons; a countermeasure. A degree of shielding would be possible from the lethal effects of DEWs, but protections are specific to weapons classes and may carry drawbacks. Heat-shield material, for example, can increase the hardness of boosters to chemical lasers, but it also reduces payload.

shoot-back: A defensive action in which a spacecraft literally shoots at its attacker.

shoot-look-shoot: A terminal-phase tactic in which fast interceptors are limited to one or two attempts at any RV.

shuttle-derived launch vehicle: A highly advanced "space truck" that could conceivably lift enormous loads of up to 150,000 pounds into space. It would have two external fuel tanks and twin booster rockets like the space shuttle, but the body would be a giant payload carrier. The United Technologies Corporation (Hartford, CT) has proposed building this type of space transport system, which it calls the unmanned payload carrier.

shuttle imaging radar (SIR): NASA's experimental device used in 1982 and 1984 to obtain radar imagery of the earth's surfaces. A synthetic aperture radar placed aboard the space shuttle was able to distinguish features 40 meters across.

shuttle-derived launch vehicle

SIDE: *See* sensor integrated discrimination experiment.

signal processing: The capability of a computer system to organize raw data received from many sources.

signature: The characteristic pattern of radiation emitted or reflected by a ballistic missile. SDI technology involves the use of signatures to identify targets and warn of early ICBM launchings. *See* discrimination.

significant technical milestones (STM) experiment: A major KEW experimental project. In September 1986 a Delta rocket was launched from Cape Canaveral, and an Aries rocket was launched from the White Sands Missile Range. The Delta put two satellites into space, one an ASAT weapon, and the other its target. The target was sought out and destroyed in a collision between it and the ASAT at 6,500 miles per hour. The Delta also contained sensors that observed the booster plume of the Aries and the upper-stage plumes of the Delta. As an exoatmospheric experiment, STM involved research into vehicle dynamics, attack guidance, ladars, and infrared sensors. The solid propellant booster plume was identified at a distance of 200 miles. *See* architecture; kinetic-energy weapons program.

silo defense: A strategic posture presented as an alternative to SDI that emphasizes the protection of ICBM silos. Silo defense would be designed primarily to enhance the survivability of land-based ICBMs, part of the U.S. offense triad, along with SLBMs and strategic bombers, but it might afford a low level of protection for some cities. Proponents argue that it would improve crisis stability by reducing the need for a launch-on-warning strategy by U.S. ICBMs, discourage Soviet thoughts of a preemptive attack, and provide a hedge against problems with other elements of the triad. *See* net defense capability; strategic defense initiative.

Skylite: The name of the field test to be conducted on the laser called MIRACL in White Sands, New Mexico.

SLBM: *See* submarine-launched ballistic missile.

SLCM: *See* sea-launched cruise missile.

slew time: The time required to reaim a defensive weapon at a new target. It also is called retarget time.

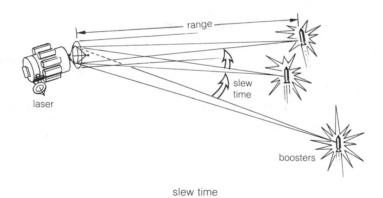

slew time

SLKT: *See* survivability, lethality, and key technologies (program).

Slocombe, Walter: Former Department of Defense official who served as the director of the SALT Task Force during the Carter administration.

"smart" rocks: Kinetic-energy projectiles that could be aimed at missiles and warheads. Equipped with homing devices, such as heat sensors, they would be launched by railguns or chemically propelled rockets. *See* electromagnetic railgun; kinetic-energy weapon.

SMES: *See* superconducting magnetic energy storage.

smoke: A countermeasure that conceals targets in the atmosphere or in space.

software: Written and printed data essential to the operation of computers. The task of coding and programming SDI will be extremely challenging, to say the least. The work will involve implementing and then coordinating the many software components. Devising a battle-management plan will be complicated by the sheer size of the job, the great number of contingencies, and the inability to pretest all programs through sufficiently realistic simulations.

Critics of SDI are calling SDI software design the most difficult task in military or civilian history. The software requirements are estimated to be three to five times more complex than those for Safeguard, which used 2 million lines of code. Computers will be needed to create the final SDI programs and test them in the national test bed. The data processing requirements could possibly be distributed among and within the defensive layers, the decentralization serving to minimize the data handling required by any subsystem. SDI also would have to investigate the effects that massive computing power would have on software development and testing.

Between 1984 and 1986, SDIO designed a set of benchmark requirements to evaluate processor performance, software engineering tools, and the defensive hardware environment. In addition, it specified the architectural requirements for fault-tolerant distributed processors, including space-qualified, radiation-hardened components. Meanwhile, SDIO asked a consortium of universities to evaluate the role of knowledge-based software assistance for battle management/C3. And SDIO is permitting its software to be integrated with DARPA's software. *See* algorithms; command and control; decentralization; security; systems analysis/battle management; testing.

sol-gel (solution-gelatin): A technological process that produces optically clear, durable, large diameter glass. The SDIO's Innovative Science and Technology Office reported this advance.

solid rocket booster (SRB): The solid-fuel booster of the space shuttle. It can lift more than 6,000 pounds into space when fitted with an appropriate upper stage.

Soviet strategic forces: The Soviets have two-thirds of their ballistic missiles mounted on 1,400 ICBMs. More than 80 percent of their

ICBM warheads are on missiles that can hold 6 to 10 warheads each. In all, they are said to have 8,000 warheads. Their silos are thought to be more hardened than those of the United States. They have in development a single-warhead ICBM and a 10-warhead ICBM (both believed mobile), a new SLBM, a long-range bomber similar to the B-1, cruise missiles, a new class of ballistic missile submarines, and a variant of their existing long-range bomber, the Bear. Between 1980 and 1985 the Soviets built 875 ICBMs, 950 SLBMs, and 2,175 theater-range ballistic missiles.

Soviet Union: In the 1980s, Soviet BMD developments have been giving the U.S. Department of Defense cause for concern. The Moscow ABM system, which the Soviets continue to develop, is a two-layered defense composed of 100 silo-based Galosh exoatmospheric interceptors and the shorter range SH-8 endoatmospheric missiles, engagement radars, and a large radar at Pushkino. The launchers may be reloadable, in violation of the ABM Treaty. Some newer defensive components might be operable in 1987.

In the Krasnoyarsk region of central Siberia—3,700 kilometers from Moscow—as well as at five other sites, the Soviets are said to be constructing large phased-array radars. The radar in Krasnoyarsk, at the town of Abalakova, is farther from Moscow than the 150 kilometers permitted by the ABM Treaty, and it is pointing outward, not inward, as specified. Moscow claims that it is for space tracking, but its design (its frequency probably will be 150 megahertz) matches those of radars at Pechora in northern Russia and at Lyaki in Azerbaijan used for ballistic missile detection and tracking. The Soviets also are reported to have developed a deployable ABM system that can be constructed in a matter of a few months, and have tested the SA-10 and SA-X-12 SAM components in an ABM mode. Near Dushanbe the Soviets supposedly are working on GBLs and might have a particle beam prototype ready by the 1990s. They have had an ASAT weapon since 1972, reportedly designed to destroy low-orbiting satellites. In addition, Soviet scientists have developed a rocket-driven magnetohydrodynamic generator, which produces 15 megawatts and a prototype for a 25-meter mirror. The generator has no counterpart in the West. The Soviet Union also could have a crude X-ray laser by 1995.

The United States is impressed with Soviet efforts in particle beams, particularly on ion sources and radio frequency quadrupole accelerators. Much laser research takes place in the Sary Shagan

Missile Test Center in Kazakhstan. The research phase of Soviet work is referred to as NIR; the design and engineering work is called OKR. Soviet space-launch sites are located deep within the Eurasian land mass at Tyuratam, Kapustin Yar, and Plesetsk. The country averages 100 launchings per year, 85 percent of which are military. The annual payload placed in orbit is ten times that of the United States, or 660,000 pounds.

	Soviet Missile Production				
	1980	*1981*	*1982*	*1983*	*1984*
ICBMs	250	200	175	150	100
LRINFs	100	100	100	125	150
SRBMs	300	300	300	350	350
SLCMs	750	750	800	800	850
SLBMs	200	175	175	200	200

SP-100: A nuclear reactor being constructed and tested by General Electric at the Hanford Development Laboratory, Hanford, Washington. Funded by SDIO, NASA, and the Department of Energy, it represents an intermediate stage of development for space-based sources of power. The SP-100 is a 100- to 300-kilowatt nuclear power system that may have the potential to grow to 1 megawatt. Cone-shaped, it stands 1 meter tall but already can provide 300 kilowatts of energy. Its major subsystems—the reactor, the power conversion system, the heat transport and radiator components (it is cooled with liquid lithium), and the control mechanism— are to be ground-tested through 1991. Launch is expected in 1993. Research

SP-100

reports indicate that thus far the SP-100 has met the long-term performance requirements of high-temperature reactor materials.

Among these it has improved the thermoelectric material used for the direct conversion of heat to electricity, and it has demonstrated that long-term unattended operations are possible.

space-based hypervelocity railgun (SBHRG): A KEW program that is to test elements of a space-based railgun. It has not been fully defined by the SDIO.

space-based kinetic-kill vehicle (SBKKV) project: A KEW project that is investigating the technology for chemically propelled space interceptors. SBKKVs represent the most mature boost intercept technology on SDI drawing boards. Until the winter of 1986, SDIO envisioned SBKKVs as the first wave of weapons in space for its comprehensive multilayered defense, recognizing that, as the Soviets developed countermeasures, the military utility of these weapons would

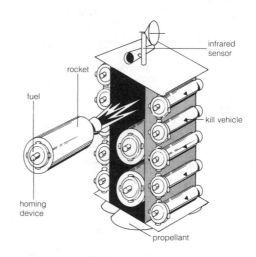

SBKKV battle station

degrade. The SBKKV project had a warhead-kill goal of perhaps 1,000. In order to achieve a 95-percent effectiveness for the entire system—and in the absence of a transition to reduced offenses— various SDI architectures called for massive deployments, by the late 1990s, of SBKKV battle stations, each housing dozens of interceptor rockets. In December 1986, however, the SDIO reoriented the project, dividing it in two: one to deploy a partially effective system within five to seven years, and the other to continue pursuing the layered defense approach.

SDI funding for 1987 indicates that the near-term deployment is getting all the attention. The near-term option in which SDIO is now engaged would have no midcourse defense, reduced sensor capabilities, and would only be able to knock out a small percentage of Soviet warheads in boost and postboost phases; the kill rate would represent only a token defense. The testing schedule for the SBKKV project has been moved up, and this has affected the requirements for space transportation. The SDIO is now leaning toward quickly developing a defensive system of 1,000 to 2,000 battle stations, each containing five 100-kilogram interceptor rockets (costing, it is hoped, only $100,000 each). SDI scientists estimate that the capabilities of such a defense would be short-lived—five to ten years as the Soviet Union developed its responsive threat. It would be effective against the SS-18 but would fail catastrophically against fast-burn boosters, to say nothing of decoys, ground-based ASAT weapons, and nuclear weapons detonations in space.

space-based laser (SBL): A space battle station with a modular assembly of laser devices and optical-phased arrays to which components could be added if the offensive threat increased. In orbit, a host station of lasers, in theory, would be able to engage ICBMs wherever launches occurred, including the ocean areas for SLBMs and Western Europe for IRBMs. SBLs also would be designed to attack postboost vehicles, destroy targets in midcourse flight, and defend U.S. satellites. Since a very bright beam could penetrate the atmosphere down to cloud tops, SBL weapons, according to SDIO, might be able to attack aircraft, cruise missiles, and tactical ballistic missiles as well.

The preferred SBL is the hydrogen fluoride-fueled chemical laser having a wavelength of 2.7 micrometers. It has been the subject of research since the late 1970s. The short-wavelength chemical laser does not appear to be viable. Other candidates for SBLs are those lasers that might generate a 1-micrometer wavelength. The radio frequency linear accelerator (RFL) free-electron laser is showing promise. The X-ray laser also has prompted interest, but it involves the introduction of nuclear weapons into space.

space-based neutral particle beam (SBNPB): A DEW concept in which negative ions are accelerated by electromagnetic fields to velocities near the speed of light. A high-energy beam supposedly then can be aimed at targets by magnets at the front of the weapon. As the ions leave the weapon, they are stripped of their negative charge, an action that allows the beam to stay together as it leaves the accelerator. Like the SBL, this space concept would make use of a configuration of battle stations for worldwide coverage. In theory, it would intercept ICBM boosters and warheads by actually penetrating the target. The SBNPB would be used in boost, postboost, and midcourse defense.

The newest—and possibly earliest—application of the SBNPB could be to discriminate warheads from decoys (interactive discrimination) during postboost and midcourse phases: primary targets would be difficult-to-distinguish decoys. The particle beam would irradiate a target, whose gamma rays and neutrons would increase in proportion to its size. A huge warhead thus would emit more radiation than a lightweight decoy or other penetration aid. The SDIO is planning a space shuttle assembly of a 100-foot neutral particle beam spacecraft in the 1990s, costing $700 million.

space detection and tracking system (SPADATS): The network of space surveillance sensors now in operation by the U.S. Air Force.

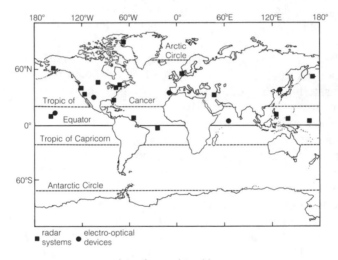

space detection and tracking system

space logistics: Enormous loads will have to be lifted into space for any SDI architecture. At present, the space shuttle is capable of carrying 30 metric tons to orbits of 200 kilometers, with less than this to higher orbits. The development of larger launch vehicles for SDI might be justified for great numbers of huge, integrated space assets. SDI proponents have advocated in-orbit assembly of defensive components, but the money this would save would depend on the size of the job. Furthermore, recovery and servicing options may require even bigger fully reusable launchers. Threats to SDI components will necessitate defenses such as protective satellites and shielding. In addition, relay and intercept mirrors for lasers would have to be checked periodically for operability, as would other components. The costs for space logistics could come to $1 trillion. *See* space transportation.

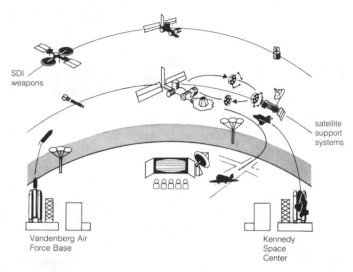

space logistics

space mines: Hypothetical devices that track and follow a target in orbit and then explode when the target is within range.

space object: The negotiator's "term of art," found in the Outer Space Treaty. The term denotes any man-made thing in space except for ballistic RVs, which were carefully exempted from the jurisdiction of the treaty.

space power: An area of research within SDI's SLKT program. Unprecedented amounts of power will be required for each SDI battle station, particularly if particle beams, railguns, or free-electron lasers are used. The power needed will be on the order of tens of megawatts; past space-based power needs have ranged from a few watts to several kilowatts. Solar power may not be sufficient. The only practical solution may lie in using nuclear systems for continuous sources, and stored chemical energy for surges. Maintenance needs, however, will have to be minimal—systems should be capable of going perhaps ten years without repair—and reliability increased, in view of the need for many battle stations. SDIO and the Department of Energy will be spending $1 billion on two chief space power programs: the SP-100 and the multimegawatt reactor.

space sanctuary: The respecting of altitude limits above which the testing or deployment of weapons by military satellites or other vehicles would be forbidden. The idea of space sanctuary could represent an element in a future ASAT and arms control agreement, but it might not constrain ASAT weapons development in space. It would enhance security by forbidding weapons tests in deep space, or above 5,600 kilometers, where critical strategic satellites might be located. This approach is less secure than a keep-out zone and more vulnerable to DEWs.

space segment: A satellite in a space system. The satellite is dependent upon its ground-based support facilities.

space station: Orbiting research facility. Initially designed for civilian purposes, the space station may still have a role in SDI. Scheduled for deployment in the mid-1990s at a cost of $13 billion—to be financed by the United States, Western Europe, Japan, and Canada—the space station was to have been used only for peaceful purposes under international agreements. In late 1986, however, the Department of Defense initiated a new defense space policy, which did not preclude manned military space operations and experiments on the space station. Projected SDI space station missions would involve technology tests only; there would be no weapons tests so as not to violate the ABM Treaty. The new policy called into question whether other nations would now join in financing and building the space station.

space station

space surveillance and tracking system (SSTS): A major SDI sensor program—part of SATKA—designed to demonstrate the space-based technology necessary to track and identify objects in the postboost, midcourse, and terminal phases. According to the Department of Defense, the SSTS would be a "near real-time" system for tracking, satellite attack warning, and verification. In the terminal phase, it would make use of the airborne optical adjunct (AOA) sensor system

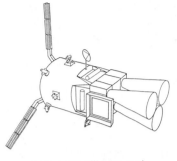

space surveillance and
tracking system

and the terminal imaging radar (TIR). (It also might be part of the U.S. ASAT weapon.) According to the SDIO, the SSTS will comply with terms of the ABM Treaty because "capabilities of any demonstration satellites will be significantly less than those necessary to achieve ABM performance levels or substitute for an ABM component."

space transportation: A research area within SDI's survivability, lethality, and kill technologies (SLKT) program. Its aim is to define and develop systems capable of lifting SDI components into space at affordable costs. The SDIO's apparent move to a near-term SDI deployment means a radical shift in U.S. plans for future space transportation. The Department of Defense is now seeking accelerated development of a heavy-lift launch vehicle (HLLV) so that it can be designed, built, tested, and ready for operations by 1992. It will be required to haul into space the space-based kinetic-kill vehicle (SBKKV) hardware at the rate of 5 million pounds annually. This represents a drastic increase from the 2 million pounds estimated beginning in 1995 under a longer term deployment of SDI. The SDIO will be trying to keep costs at $200 to $400 per pound launched into space, but critics contend that this is not possible.

Other transportation systems the SDIO is investigating include the shuttle-derived vehicle; the Shuttle II, a follow-on to the space

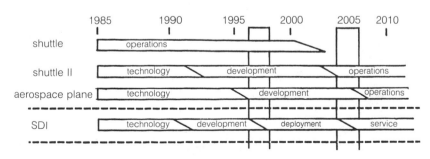

space transportation

shuttle that might be ready by 2005; expendable lift vehicles; and the national aerospace plane, a hypersonic aircraft that would take off from the United States, fly into space, and land in Asia.

Spartan: The nuclear-armed, long-range interceptor that was part of the Safeguard ABM system. It was designed to detonate above the atmosphere, destroying several RVs at once. Its range was several hundred miles.

specific impulse: A measure of a rocket's performance, indicating how long it takes 1 pound of fuel to produce 1 pound of thrust. The longer the time (measured in seconds), the hotter the engine is. Solid propellants usually result in a higher specific impulse. In general, U.S. rockets have higher specific impulses than Soviet systems.

spin-offs: Any nonmilitary applications of SDI—lasers in medicine, gallium arsenide in computer technology—which critics deride as small benefits for exorbitant investments.

spoofing: The use of misleading signals or decoys to defeat sensors in an SDI architecture.

Sprint: The nuclear-armed, short-range interceptor in the Safeguard ABM system. As a fast-burning, terminal-phase interceptor, it had a range of only 25 miles.

SRB: *See* solid rocket booster.

SS-18: The largest Soviet ICBM, credited with carrying ten RVs, and capable of holding perhaps fourteen. It is supposed to have eight times the throw-weight of the U.S. Minuteman III, which has been tested with seven warheads. There are 308 such missiles in the Soviet arsenal.

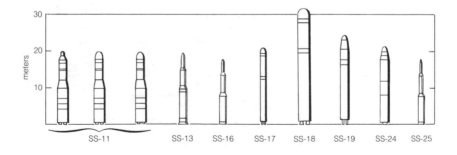

SS-18

SS-19: A liquid-fueled Soviet ICBM that carries six RVs and has one-half of the throw-weight of the SS-18.

SS-20: An intermediate-range Soviet missile. There are 810 warheads on 270 such missiles in Europe, and 500 warheads on SS-20s located in Asia. This missile remains an issue between U.S. and Soviet arms control negotiators.

SS-24: The new ten-warhead Soviet missile permitted under the ABM Treaty. (The new U.S. missile is the MX.)

SS-25: A solid-fueled, three-stage, single-warhead missile, which the Soviets say is a replacement for their SS-13. The United States contends instead that the SS-25 is actually a new system not permitted by the ABM Treaty. In response, the United States is developing the Midgetman missile.

SS-NX-21: The Soviet cruise missile deployed aboard submarines.

SSTS: *See* space surveillance and tracking system.

Standing Consultative Commission (SCC): A U.S.-Soviet body charged with implementing the SALT agreements, particularly compliance problems. However, neither nation really relies on it greatly.

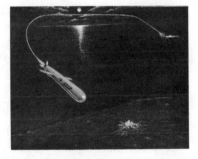

SS-NX-21

stand-off weapon: A weapon on board an ASAT that would be capable of inflicting damage at a great distance. It could be a KEW, a laser, a particle beam accelerator, or an isotropic warhead.

Starlab: A space tracking and pointing experiment in the SDIO's technology integration program that would make use of shuttle-launched vehicles.

STEP: *See* Surveillance Tracking and Experiment Program.

stimulated emission: *See* emission, stimulated.

STM: *See* significant technical milestones (experiment).

Strategic Arms Limitation Talks (SALT I and II): The series of arms control negotiations between the United States and the Soviet

Union from November 1969 through 1979, which culminated in several important agreements. In May 1972 the two nations signed the ABM Treaty, and the Interim Agreement, which limited the number of ICBM and SLBM launchers for five years. In 1979, SALT II set further limits on ICBMs, SLBM launchers, and intercontinental-range bombers. It also established several sublimits on multiple-warhead launchers and prohibited the two parties from developing, testing, or deploying "systems for placing into earth orbit nuclear weapons." Conservatives in the United States opposed the ratification of SALT II; therefore, the treaty was never ratified by the U.S. Senate. The Soviet Union also never ratified it, but both nations adhered to its provisions until late 1986 when the United States exceeded the limitations imposed by SALT II on delivery vehicles. Furthermore, the United States indicated it might abandon the ABM Treaty. Until this time the Soviet Union had replaced or dismantled more than 1,200 launchers or nuclear weapons to stay within the limits of the Interim Agreement and SALT II.

There were disputes, however, within the U.S. defense establishment over whether Soviet encryption of telemetry data complied with treaty provisions, and whether the Soviets were in violation of SALT II provisions that allowed only one new type of land-based missile. Also subject to differing interpretations was the total number of delivery vehicles allowed by the treaty. Almost since the beginning the Reagan administration had been saying it would not adhere to the provisions of SALT II. *See* ABM Treaty.

strategic defense: A national or international defense posture that depends on weapons that can shoot down other weapons. Currently, SDI is not included in the U.S. strategic posture. Air defenses at this time are minimal, although they are being upgraded. However, the Reagan administration differs from its predecessors in its conception of the role that BMD might play in nuclear strategy, and in its planning for BMD research and development. A decision on the actual incorporation of SDI defenses may not come before the completion of BMD research, which could take ten years. Then, the United States would decide what to do. On the other hand, it could come much earlier—perhaps 1988—if pressure for early deployment continues. *See* deployment.

strategic defense initiative (SDI): The Department of Defense program that explores the promise of BMD as envisioned in a March

1983 speech by President Ronald Reagan. Among the most vital goals of SDI is the possible encouragement of deep reductions in nuclear arsenals by the United States and the Soviet Union. One scenario outlines these steps to arms cuts: a program to explore BMD architectures, the deployment of which might turn out to be cheaper than a continued arms buildup; a decision in the 1990s to develop such defenses by the year 2000; negotiations with the Soviets for agreed mutual deployment of defenses, cou-

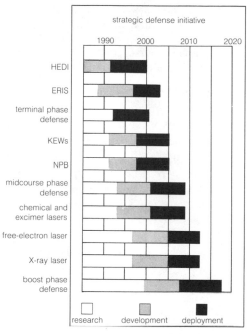

strategic defense initiative

pled with reductions in offensive weapons so that the chance of nuclear war, while not completely eliminated, is reduced; and an ultimate stage in which BMD, air defenses, and negotiated reductions of offensive weapons to extremely low levels will have eliminated the need for deterrence and the threat of mutual assured destruction.

Under SDI, the defense shifts from older BMD technologies, based on nuclear-armed interceptors guided by radar, to newer and potentially more powerful technologies. SDI activities have been grouped into five chief elements, encompassing sixteen major experiments that have BMD applications: SATKA, DEWs, KEWs, SLKT, and SA/BM. The SDIO is asking the U.S. scientific and academic communities to participate (*see* IST program), and it also is exploring defenses against the shorter range ballistic missiles, particularly those targeted against Europe. SDI may be the most expensive and research-intensive military program ever undertaken. In 1984, it employed nearly 5,000 scientists, technicians, and engineers; in 1987 the figure is expected to triple. Some say that, if SDI were designed to include both air and civil defenses, it would offer the best—and perhaps only plausable—prospect for a dramatic reduction in the nuclear threat to American society.

Strategic Defense Initiative Institute: Proposed research and development center that would support the SDIO.

Strategic Defense Initiative Organization (SDIO): A Department of Defense agency, chartered in 1984 and headed by Lt. Gen. James Abrahamson, that is responsible for the five-year SDI program. The SDIO has established a three-part program to oversee the SDI effort: basic and applied technology research, feasibility experiments on potential SDI components, and demonstration-of-capabilities projects of technologies deemed feasible. The SDIO works with the following agencies or organizations: the U.S. Army's Strategic Defense Command, U.S. Air Force Headquarters, the Defense Nuclear Agency, the Department of Energy, the Defense Advanced Research Projects Agency, national laboratories (Lawrence Livermore, Los Alamos, Sandia), and numerous private organizations

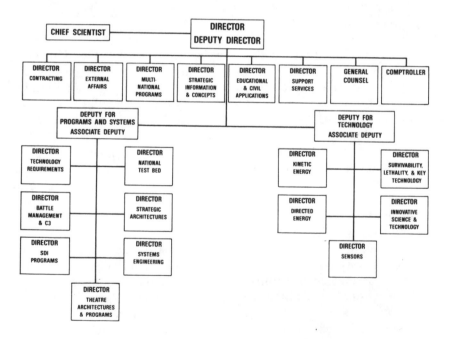

Strategic Defense Initiative Organization

that have received more than 1,000 contracts since 1985. The SDIO has roughly one hundred staffers, with about one-half of them military personnel. The director of SDIO reports to the secretary of defense.

strategic forces: *See* strategic weapons.

strategic reserve: The SLBMs are the most stabilizing leg of the U.S. defense triad of land-based missiles, submarine-launched ballistic missiles, and bombers because of their relative invulnerability to preemptive attack.

strategic stability: The doctrine of strategic balance between the United States and the Soviet Union that encompasses crisis stability and arms control stability. Some conservatives argue that the United States and its allies should be prepared to meet a possible attack by the Soviet Union with massive retaliation and still ensure the survival of the West. But the current official U.S. concept of strategic stability makes no reference to U.S. ability to inflict massive societal damage on the Soviet Union. The newer concept of strategic stability aims at preventing a catastrophe rather than trying to avenge one. At the same time, however, the United States does not seem to question the bizarre notion that the Soviet Union's unrestricted offensive-weapons access to the United States somehow enhances international security. The Soviet Union, it seems, is an ardent advocate of homeland defense—as it ably and heroically demonstrated in World War II—as long as it is not American homeland defense. *See* strategic defense initiative.

strategic weapons: Nuclear weapons having intercontinental range; weapons that are capable of reaching the Soviet Union. The Soviets consider any U.S. nuclear weapon capable of landing on its territory part of the U.S. arsenal of strategic forces.

submarine-launched ballistic missile (SLBM): This kind of missile and the IRBM have trajectories that are similar in boost and terminal phases to that of an ICBM, but they have less extensive postboost and midcourse phases. SLBMs can fly in trajectories at such low angles that their entire flight, not just the boost phase, would be within the protective blanket of the atmosphere. The missiles could not be intercepted by any SDI defenses thus far imagined, with the possible exception of the long-wave chemical lasers and KEW interceptors in the terminal phase. *See* architecture.

supercapacitor: A still theoretical device that would permit the storage of 250 kilojoules of energy in the same container that now holds only a single-kilojoule capacitor. SDI's goal is to store a megajoule of energy in this container within three years. If this can be accomplished, capacitors could begin to compete with the more complex SDI schemes for the economic storage of power in space.

superconducting magnetic energy storage (SMES): A theoretical source of power for ground-based free-electron lasers being investigated by scientists calling themselves the Wisconsin Team (University of Wisconsin, Madison Gas & Electric, and Ebasco Services). The team is seeking funding from the SDIO to build a $60-million prototype that could deliver 20 megawatts of power in five years. The source of power would be a coil of niobium-titanium wire submerged in liquid helium.

superfluorescence: *See* superradiance.

superradiance: The process used by a superradiant laser to generate or amplify a laser beam in a single pass through a lasant material, or—as in the case of a free-electron laser—through the electric or magnetic field in the presence of an electron beam. This phenomenon is a form of stimulated emission, also known as amplified spontaneous emission, or superfluorescence.

support programs: The SDI's DEW program that funds activities of the HELSTF at White Sands Missile Range and the DEW portion of the IST program.

supreme national interest: An escape clause found in most defense treaties of unlimited duration, which allows the parties to withdraw if they deem the nation's future is at stake.

surveillance, acquisition, tracking, and kill assessment (SATKA): A major SDI program, studying data-gathering techniques as they apply to ballistic missiles and warheads. The program is examining new radar and optical sensors capable of obtaining detailed imagery of warheads and warhead deployment as well as studying on-board signal and data processing. Planned experiments will involve the use of sensors for boost-phase surveillance, midcourse tracking, and terminal-phase discrimination. The SATKA program comprises the BSTS, the SSTS, the AOA, and the TIR experiments. In the area of infrared sensors, cryocoolers are being developed to make sensing more accurate. Gallium arsenide pilot projects are under way in signal processing, and an advanced distributed on-board processor has been installed at the Advanced Research Institute, Huntsville, Alabama. By the early 1990s this program is supposed to be able to detect and track boosters from high altitudes and to track thousands of objects during midcourse flight,

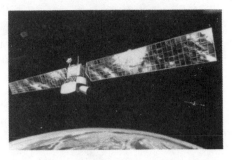

surveillance, acquisition, tracking, and kill assessment

something that now seems inconceivable. Another experiment will determine the feasibility of using optical sensors for discrimination. *See* airborne optical adjunct; boost surveillance and tracking system; space surveillance and tracking system; terminal imaging radar.

surveillance and acquisition: Sensing and detection is a task of any layered SDI architecture. All enemy attacks would have to be detected, and the number, location, and destination of threatening targets determined. Reported progress in the miniaturizing of components, as well as advances in optical sensors, has improved in surveillance technologies. SDI research has proven that radar and optical sensors can be used to obtain multispectral measurements of a booster, a postboost vehicle, and RV signatures. These measurements may allow a better understanding of threat signatures and will be used in the further development of sensors. The hardening of high-density microelectronic processors and infrared focal-plane arrays enhance these components' survival during battle.

Surveillance Tracking and Experiment Program (STEP): A proposed $600-million space experiment for 1989–90 that was to have involved a prototype space surveillance and tracking system (SSTS) tracking a postboost vehicle and midcourse objects. The experiment was canceled in 1987, implying that the SDIO is shelving, for the moment, the midcourse discrimination mission.

survivability: Ability to withstand attack. SDI defenses, particularly space-based weapons platforms, may themselves be vulnerable to attack. After all, technology used to destroy missiles also can be used against defensive components in space. Passive and active measures could improve survivability. These would include the hiding of satellites in distant orbits or very close ones, hardening, the proliferation of satellites and the use of decoys, the jamming of enemy sensors, spoofing, and the use of armed defensive satellites.

		Survivability of Lasers		
	SBL (Pulsed)	SBL (Repetitive, Continuous)	GBL	GBL (with Mirrors)
Against attack	no	yes	no	yes
Against countermeasures	no	yes	yes	yes
Cost to attack	high	high	low	low
Laser can attack target	yes	yes	no	no
Need for space surveillance for targeting	no	yes	yes	yes

survivability, lethality, and key technologies (SLKT) program: An SDI research program focusing on the vulnerability of defensive weapons to attack; the system requirements for space transportation, space power, and multimegajoule energy storage and conversion. It funds research to develop technologies and tactics to ensure the survivability of SDI defenses; reduce the uncertainties in attacking offensive targets; stimulate the development of energy generation, conversion, and power for space; create the initial technologies for space transportation, repair, and resupply; and develop other unique materials and structures. There are six projects in the program: system vulnerability, lethality and target hardening, space power and conditioning, space transportation and support, materials and structures development, and countermeasures.

survivable space capability: The protection afforded satellites by hardening against radiation, system-generated electromagnetic pulse, and nuclear effects. Hardening and other measures would be allowed under the ABM Treaty in the absence of an ASAT ban.

"swarm-jet proposal": A kinetic-energy, terminal-phase technique, whereby many interceptors are fired at an incoming RV. If properly timed and aimed at a region 50 meters in diameter at a range of 1 kilometer from the defending site, the swarm can be successful, provided that the attacking warhead is not salvage-fused.

SWIR: short-wave infrared. *See* electromagnetic radiation.

synthetic aperture radar (SAR): A radar technique that picks up the echoes of signals emitted at different points along a satellite's orbit.

system survivability: An area of research within the SLKT program meant to ensure the survival of any SDI system developed and deployed. It assists in the development of any architecture and investigates all avenues of survival for BMD, including the possibility of attempting to overwhelm the defense. Within the last two years, SDI has investigated the hardening of electronic components and subsystems from the effects of nuclear radiation and other environmental conditions. It has developed devices to protect electronics from an electromagnetic pulse; it is hardening optical surfaces against similar effects; and it continues to test the effects of radio waves on electronics. Finally, SDI is looking at the area of counter-countermeasures. *See* counter-countermeasure; survivability

systems analysis/battle management (SA/BM): The SDI effort that will examine competing approaches to defense architectures and that will develop battle management/C3 systems. The systems analysis process starts with the definition of a defensive system architecture into which various technologies may be integrated. Once an architecture has been chosen, performance requirements for the subsystems must be defined. Then, the offensive and defensive tactics have to be evaluated, including possible defense-suppression attacks and enemy defense-avoidance tactics.

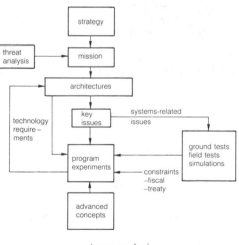

systems analysis

Within the systems analysis project are four subgroups: architecture, threat analysis, technology-integration, and architecture analysis support.

At the project's completion, SDI must finally be structured to meet the technical performance requirements defined by the architecture and resolve all key technology-related or system-related issues. This must be done by the early 1990s when a decision on whether to deploy SDI is expected to be made. (The SDIO has not indicated how this systems analysis/battle-management effort will be affected by an early deployment of SDI.) The battle-management effort defines the operational environment of decisions, rules, constraints, and directions in which individual systems must perform. *See* architecture; battle management; command and control; communications.

systems architecture and tradeoff study: *See* horserace acquisition studies.

tactical: When referring to delivery systems, this term applies to short-range systems used on the battlefield. The United States has about 5,000 tactical weapons, including nuclear weapons, in Europe.

tactical ballistic missile (TBM): Any defense against TBMs would be the same as that in a terminal-phase defense of a layered SDI architecture.

tail: Military slang for the rocket engine of a ballistic missile.

tail wagging: The condition that occurs when swiveled or gimballed ballistic missile rocket engines experience moments of inertia. The dynamics of a ballistic missile are such that the missile can be treated as rigid. It will actually experience destabilization because of the effects of body bending and its fuel sloshing around in the tanks.

talon gold: An experimental program within the SDIO's DEW project that has increased researchers' confidence in pointing beam weapons with extreme precision. Hardware used in the experiment is to be part of the tracking and pointing tests on the space shuttle.

target destruction: One of the most important tasks of a layered SDI system. Target destruction means that the defensive weapons would have to deliver rapid and sufficient energy against targets.

targeting: The territory and assets threatened by an enemy in a nuclear exchange. Since the sequence in which targets would be struck is not known, the relationship between target planning and the rest of strategic policymaking is complicated. SDI planners will have to take into consideration the vulnerability of SDI to attack and the defensive postures that might be employed to protect ICBM silos. *See* defense.

TBM: *See* tactical ballistic missile.

teal ruby sensor: This is to be a space-based surveillance system capable of detecting and tracking aircraft near the earth's surface. It is a focal-plane mosaic array that will eventually contain 100,000 infrared detectors. It is scheduled to be deployed by the space shuttle within the next few years.

teal ruby sensor

technology-based development: An SDI project within its DEW program that will explore the technology of beam generation needed for acquisition, tracking, pointing, and fire control. This is to involve the focusing and propagating of lasers of various wavelengths and of neutral particle beams, the acquiring of targets for beams by establishing lines of sight, and the fixing of beams on targets. In addition, the program will assess damage and look at the use of nuclear DEWs. *See* X-ray laser.

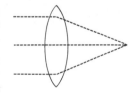

technology-based development: NPB focusing lens

technology-integration experiments: An SDI project within its DEW program that will perform proof-of-feasibility testing on the free-electron laser, investigate the possibility of interactive discrimination by a neutral particle beam, and validate space-pointing and tracking experiments. There also may be some work on non-DEW concepts such as Starlab and Pathfinder.

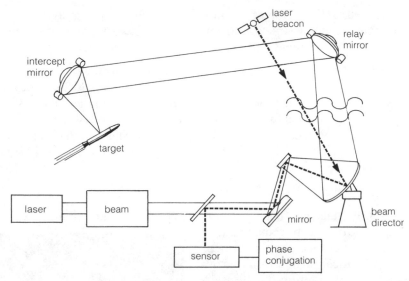

technology-integration experiments

technology push: What is seen as possible; one way in which technological evolution influences strategy. (The other is called requirements pull, or that which is viewed to be necessary.) Technology push is a major motivational factor for supporters of SDI, who believe that the United States can now develop considerably more sophisticated defenses than were thought possible even a few years ago.

telemetry: The technology of automatic measurement and transmission of data from a space vehicle to a receiving station for analysis. The data can reveal a weapon's characteristics and performance. There are two kinds of data. Payload data is information about a complete mission, while state-of-health data deals with the operational status of a satellite and its equipment. Satellite telemetry involves measurements by a satellite's remote sensors.

telemetry, tracking, and commanding (TTC): The three functions used to control a satellite. A satellite requires TTC to locate and track it, communicate with it, guide it, and obtain data from it.

Teller, Edward: A strong advocate of SDI, particularly of the X-ray laser. Teller was a founder of the Lawrence Livermore National Laboratory. Because of his work on fusion, he is known as the Father of the Hydrogen Bomb.

10-kilojoule criterion: A physical standard that stipulates that 10,000 joules of energy, or fluence, applied properly will destroy almost anything. This criterion—basic to the development of weapons for SDI—is based on two premises: the vaporization of 1 gram of almost anything requires approximately 10 kilojoules, and the removal of 1 gram of material (1 centimeter cubed) from a vital spot in a target will destroy the target. According to this rule, a practicable DEW would have to deliver a minimum of 10 kilojoules to a target volume 1 centimeter cubed in a time span that is too short for the target to get rid of the energy. The formula that expresses the relationship among the variables that would affect the utility of lasers and other directed energy is:

$$f = (2r)(2r)mt/10(w)(w)(d)(d),$$

where

f is the energy required to destroy a target, expressed in kilojoules
r is the radius of the laser's mirror, expressed in meters
m is the power of the laser, expressed in megawatts
t is the dwell time
w is the laser's wavelength, expressed in microns
d is the distance to a target, expressed in megameters

See laser; particle beam.

terminal imaging radar (TIR): A major SDI research program that will evaluate a BMD radar in a fixed ground-based mode. It is part of the experimental program called SATKA. In a terminal-phase defense, the TIR would be used to discriminate RVs from decoys and send information to the interceptor missile designated as HEDI. The radar also could receive hand-over data from the airborne optical adjunct

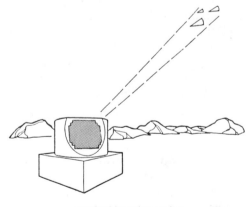

terminal imaging radar

(AOA). Appropriations for this program were slated to be $49 million, but the program's funding was slashed to $29 million in 1985.

The TIR radar will be an X-band ABM radar, to be tested in an ABM mode at Kwajalein Missile Range. *See* sensor, active.

terminal phase: The final defensive phase in an SDI-layered architecture. In this phase the defense would have only about 1 minute or so to intercept any remaining warheads about to reenter the

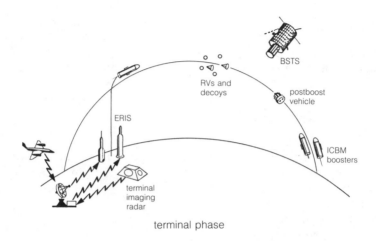

terminal phase

atmosphere. These RVs would be set to explode when they reached their targets. The idea of a terminal defense was a very divisive issue around the time of the ABM Treaty; it now has more appeal because SDI researchers claim better detection, discrimination, tracking, and interception methods. In addition, if hardened sites were being defended, intercepts could occur at low altitude because hardened targets, by definition, would be designed to survive nearby nuclear explosions. Only a few seconds would be available to the defense to launch ERIS and HEDI missiles in this phase, but it would have had 30 minutes or so to get ready to engage RVs if the other layers of the SDI architecture handed off trajectory information to it.

The surveillance functions that this phase would make use of are airborne optical sensors, which would have to detect RVs; the terminal imaging radar (TIR); and perhaps low-energy lasers. Some advocates of a terminal phase, particularly Edward Teller, have suggested using small, defensive nuclear weapons to destroy RVs. The "advantages" would be reliability, the need for less accuracy, and the possibility that the RVs also could be carrying biological agents. (The Soviet Union was said to be experimenting with deadly pulmonary anthrax in the early 1980s.) *See* architecture; ballistic missile defense; deployment.

tested in an ABM mode: An ABM Treaty limitation, specifying that an interceptor is considered "tested in an ABM mode" if it has attempted to intercept a strategic ballistic missile. Also, a radar in an ABM mode is considered to have been tested in the same fashion if it tracks and guides an ABM interceptor missile, a strategic ballistic missile, or any of their elements.

testing: The complexity of SDI will mean that full system software and hardware testing will be impossible. In fact, SDI may be too complex to succeed. Since the realistic testing of the entire system has no complete technical solution, the credibility of the system may have to be established by researchers evaluating all subsystems and functions separately through the national test bed. It should be kept in mind that the testing of some features of SDI would constitute a violation of the ABM Treaty. Full-blown tests in space, for instance, of DEWs and associated hardware would be one such violation. Some opponents of SDI have suggested the testing of sensor systems only, but not weapons, in order to remain within treaty limits. Even if SDI were successfully deployed, it might fail under attack conditions because of inadequate and improper testing, or it might even start under a false alarm. Then, with little time available in a layered defense, SDI would be releasing weapons automatically; technicians could not be expected to uncover all faults during a possible threat condition. *See* national test bed.

theater: A region or theater of operations.

thermal blooming: A phenomenon that can disturb or defocus the propagation of a laser beam through the atmosphere. As a laser heats the air through which it passes, the atmospheric molecules absorb some of its energy. This absorption will reduce the power of the laser. Theoretically, thermal blooming could be controlled by phase-compensation techniques, or by changing the wavelengths of the laser.

thermal conductivity: A measure of a substance's capacity to conduct heat. Thermal conductivity is not important in charged particle beam interactions. However, it is critical for lasers, which deposit their energy on a target's surface. *See* 10-kilojoule criterion.

thermal kill: One way, theoretically, by which a DEW would destroy or disable a target. Intense heat at a level of 10 to 100 kilojoules, deposited onto 1 cubic centimeter of the target, could lead to structural failure of its components. The heat, however, must be delivered quickly; if it takes too long, the heated area of the booster may cool and dissipate the heat. *See* 10-kilojoule criterion.

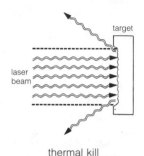

thermal kill

thermoplastic resins: Materials containing discrete polymer molecules that will repeatedly soften when heated and harden when cooled. These kinds of substances can be polyethylenes, vinyls, nylons, and fluorocarbons. *See* polymer-matrix composites.

third-generation weapon: A DEW, such as the X-ray laser, whose pumping source involves an atom bomb (a first-generation weapon) or a hydrogen bomb (a second-generation weapon). This type of weapon makes use of the energy of the explosion—the waves of energy expanding outward—before it is destroyed itself. *See* X-ray laser.

THOR: *See* tiered hierarchy overlayed research.

threat: The total number of weapons which an enemy might have. Threat would include nuclear weapons and their delivery systems, decoys, penetration aids, and BMD countermeasures.

threat cloud: The number of RVs and decoys that the postboost phase or midcourse phase of an SDI architecture would encounter.

Threshold Test Ban Treaty: The 1974 treaty, not yet ratified by the U.S. Senate, that prohibits aboveground testing of nuclear weapons with a yield greater than 150 kilotons.

throw-weight: The payload, or the combined weight, of the warheads, guidance systems, decoys, and penetration aids carried by a missile. Throw-weight is a major indicator of the military strength of strategic forces.

tiered hierarchy overlayed research (THOR): A proposed series of tests of space-based kinetic-kill vehicles. The Department of Defense has indicated that the first experiments could take place in 1988.

TIR: *See* terminal imaging radar.

Titan Corporation: A defense contractor, based in La Jolla, California, whose work includes designs for U.S. communications satellites, computers, and DEWs.

Tomahawk: A U.S. sea-launched cruise missile. The total number of warheads for the Tomahawk may reach 700 by 1988.

TPE: *See* tracking and pointing experiments.

TPS-43E: A highly advanced U.S. ground-based surveillance radar. An improved version for SDI applications could cost about $500 million.

track file: Information stored in computer memory about the trajectories, positions, coordinates, and velocities of targets. The track file also would contain data about boosters, RVs, decoys, and penetration aids.

tracking: The monitoring of targets' azimuth, elevation, and range. In each layer of a BMD defense the actual and predicted positions of targets are required for interception. The tracking system, which would be continually updated with new information, also receives telemetry data to help determine paths and orbits of targets.

tracking and pointing experiments (TPE): SDI experiments that involve the use of lasers to track satellites and rockets. These experiments are scheduled to be part of the space shuttle program in 1988. *See* pointing and tracking; tracking.

trajectory, depressed: *See* trajectory, low-flight.

trajectory, lofted: The flight path of an ICBM from the Soviet Union to the United States, having a flight time of about 40 minutes, an apogee at 2,300 kilometers, and a reentry angle of 35 degrees. The flight time for a missile in a lofted trajectory would last longer than would other trajectories, but reentry takes place at a faster speed and at less of an angle. *See* ballistic missile.

trajectory, low-flight: The flight path of an ICBM (or a decoy) from the Soviet Union to the United States, having a flight time of about 30 minutes, an apogee at 900 kilometers, and a reentry angle of 15 degrees. A low-flight trajectory also is called a depressed trajectory because the ICBM booster stays within the atmosphere until burnout. In this way it would be protected by the atmosphere from some

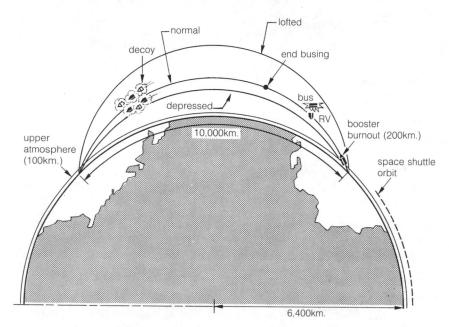

trajectory: lofted, low-flight, and minimum energy

types of DEWs. In addition, its reentry angle would be a difficult one for SDI sensors to pick up. *See* ballistic missile.

trajectory, minimum energy: This would be the normal flight path of an ICBM from the Soviet Union to the United States, lasting about 30 minutes. It allows the booster to carry the maximum number of RVs and decoys while using the least amount of fuel. The reentry angle would be 23 degrees, and apogee would occur at 1,200 kilometers. *See* ballistic missile.

transition: The period during which the world strategic balance would shift from an offense-dominated to a defense-dominated posture. In reducing the threat of nuclear destruction, this would be a major arms control gain coming out of SDI. However, it is seen by some arms control experts as extremely difficult to negotiate, and perhaps not possible. The problem of passing through such a period has been called tricky by Paul Nitze. It has been described as a potential source of instability; the premium for striking first, and the penalty for waiting, could be powerful destabilizing factors, particularly during an acute crisis. During such a transition the United States or the Soviet Union might see some "advantage" in a first strike. On the other hand, could any government and its people—for whatever reason—live with the knowledge of having started a nuclear war?

A further consideration for arms control experts would be how to verify a transition agreement. Precautions by both sides during this period could include passive defense and a shift from present arsenals to bombers and cruise missiles. Given what the Reagan administration says is at stake over SDI—the physical protection of the American people and their allies—and the absence of an attractive, attainable alternative, the case for trying to achieve a transition has strong appeal. As an inducement to negotiations, some have argued for following twin paths of negotiating and upgrading U.S. military programs because, for the next few years, the Soviet Union will almost certainly shun negotiations on reductions of strategic offense that would lend credence to U.S. efforts with SDI.

A period of transition will have to be earned at the negotiating table. After twenty years it might not be in sight. (What appears self-evident to the engineer and technician may simply be wishful thinking that the Soviets should realize that their interest lies in cooperating with the United States over a transition.) Then again, it also can be argued that the Soviet Union would reduce its offensive threat if it sees the United States proceeding with both SDI and the development and deployment of new offensive systems that would diminish Soviet security. In other words, if the Soviets believe that SDI works and that their defenses might not work as well, then they might consider a transition agreement. SDI would then lead to a functional disarmament of ICBMs. Actual disarmament would follow when the Soviet Union concluded that the delivery of weapons was unreliable and perhaps futile. *See* arms control policy.

triad: The U.S. strategic forces composed of ICBMs, SLBMs, and nuclear bombers.

tribology: The study of the phenomenon and mechanisms of friction, lubrication, and the wear of surfaces in relative motion. *See* composite.

Trident: The U.S. sea-based missiles. The total number of warheads for such missiles is 2,600.

Tsipis, Kosta: MIT professor who is an opponent of SDI. Tsipis has calculated that it would take years to lift enough fuel into space to support a space-based laser BMD.

TTC: *See* telemetry, tracking, and commanding.

u

UCAM: United Campuses to Prevent Nuclear War is a Washington, DC, based organization that has circulated a petition urging a boycott of SDI by university science and engineering departments. Organizers claim that one-half of all science and engineering faculty at the nation's top ten universities have agreed not to participate in SDI research.

underfly: Literally, to get "below" any SDI architecture by using aircraft, cruise missiles, or SLBMs.

undulator: A wiggler, or modulated magnetic field, used by free-electron lasers. *See* free-electron laser.

Union of Concerned Scientists: An organization of scientists, based in Cambridge, Massachusetts, that opposes SDI research. The organization's studies indicate that a space-based laser system would require 1,300 tons of fuel to be sent into space at a cost of $4 billion.

U.S. strategic forces: These forces number about 1,000 ICBMs, 600 SLBMs, and 325 long-range bombers carrying gravity bombs, short-range attack missiles, and air-launched cruise missiles (ALCM). Six thousand (or three-quarters) of the country's ballistic missile warheads are deployed on SLBMs. No U.S. ICBM now carries more than three warheads. The country is building the ten-warhead MX ICBM, the B-1 bomber, the SLCM, and the Trident I (C-4) SLBM. In various stages of development are the small single-warhead Midgetman ICBM (possibly for mobile deployment), an advanced technology "stealth" bomber, an advanced ALCM, and the Trident II (D-5) SLBM. The total number of U.S. nuclear warheads is 25,000.

Utgoff, Victor A.: Coauthor with Barry M. Blechman of a widely circulated study on strategic defense. *See* Blechman, Barry M.

utility: The value placed on a military satellite. A satellite having a high utility could provide timely information, speedy communications, surveillance of closed areas, and early warning of launches.

UV: ultraviolet. *See* electromagnetic radiation.

D

van Allen belt: A belt of radiation around the earth. Radiation pumped into this region by nuclear bursts would affect sensors and electronic circuits of SDI components.

Vandenberg Air Force Base: The California launching site of the space shuttle for satellites whose orbits must take them over the earth's poles. This kind of orbit is not possible from the shuttle pad at the Kennedy Space Center in Florida. Shuttle flights were to have included six SDI tests per year beginning in 1986, but the *Challenger* disaster in January 1986 altered schedules and test plans. If shuttle flights resume by 1988 (the first tracking and pointing experiment is now scheduled for mid-1988), SDI will have four to five years to experiment before a decision is made whether or not to develop SDI. However, the SDI schedule may be altered if the Air Force mothballs Vandenberg AFB—as it said it wished to do in mid-1986—until 1991 or 1992.

verification: The monitoring of agreements. Verification is a demanding and sometimes neglected aspect of arms control agreements because it can be more difficult to discuss verification in negotiations than it actually is to achieve in terms of technology used. To discuss it successfully, it is necessary to determine what aspects of strategy one wants to control and then to establish meaningful criteria for judging how closely to monitor potential constraints. *See* national technical means (of verification).

vulnerability: The inverse of survivability. The characteristics of a space system that cause it to suffer degradation because of a hostile environment. Vulnerability usually would apply only to a single segment or element of a space-based BMD. Of particular interest to SDI researchers will be the lowest level at which the effects of degradation are acceptable to SDI components. *See* system survivability.

Vyssotsky, Victor: Director of information science at Bell Laboratories, Murray Hill, New Jersey. Vyssotsky was responsible for the development of software for the Sentinel/Safeguard ABM system and has stated that it is feasible to develop software for SDI. *See* software.

warhead: A nuclear weapon contained in the payload of a missile.

watt: One joule per second.

weapons, high-power radio frequency: *See* high-power radio frequency weapons.

weapons platform: Any satellite, rocket, or projectile that would carry a weapon in an SDI architecture.

West Germany: This nation has signed agreements with the United States to make it easier for West German firms to participate in SDI research. By the end of 1986, SDI research grants to West Germany had reached $50 million. The amounts to representative firms were $38 million to Messerschmitt-Bolkow-Blohm, which is building a weapons platform and designing infrared sensors; $4 million to Dornier, which is developing instrument pointing devices for lasers and sensors; $4 million to Interatom, which is doing laser research; $1 million to Schott Optical Glass, which is fabricating lightweight laser relay and intercept mirrors; and about $0.5 million to Carl Zeiss, which is researching laser imaging radars.

wiggler: A modulated magnetic field or undulator. Used in the free-electron laser, it can be 90 feet or longer. *See* accelerator; free-electron laser.

Wood, Lowell: An outspoken physicist on nuclear weapons design at the Lawrence Livermore National Laboratory. Wood is a strong advocate of SDI and the X-ray laser, and he is a protégé of Edward Teller.

World-Wide Military Command and Control System (WWMCCS): The communications network linking U.S. forces.

WSMR: The White Sands Missile Range, located in New Mexico. It is one of two sites for the testing of defensive systems in an ABM mode.

X

Xraser: The X-ray laser. It also stands for the computer code designed by Peter Hagelstein in 1979 that described the physics of the X-ray laser. The program contained 40,000 lines of code.

X-ray: Electromagnetic radiation having wavelengths shorter than 10 nanometers. It is electromagnetic radiation that results from the release of energy from electrons changing orbits about the nucleus or the inelastic collision of charged particles with the electromagnetic field of the nucleus.

X-ray laser: The still theoretical, expendable, single-shot laser that would generate electromagnetic radiation at wavelengths of less than 10 nanometers (10 billionths of a meter, or 100 angstroms). It also is called the Xraser or XRL. The U.S. government has released little information about its efforts to use the energy of nuclear power in a DEW. Although President Ronald Reagan has insisted that SDI is to consider only the use of nonnuclear weapons, Washington continues in its efforts to harness the power of a directed beam of X-rays from a nuclear source. Such a device would constitute a third generation of nuclear weapons, after atomic and hydrogen.

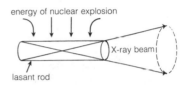

energy of nuclear explosion

X-ray beam

lasant rod

X-ray laser

The X-ray laser would use the same amount of energy as atomic and hydrogen weapons but would conceivably be able to direct more of that energy toward an ascending booster, rather than allowing it to escape in all directions. Its design would be simple: thin fibers of lasing material would be powered, or pumped, by intense pulsed radiation. The radiant heat of a nuclear explosion would raise electrons of the atoms of a lasant to upper-energy levels. As the electrons fall back to lower levels of energy, lasing would occur. (The chemical nature of the lasant has not been revealed by the U.S. government.) The resulting laser beam would diverge at an angle roughly equal to the square root of the wavelength divided by the square root of the length of the fiber. It would have to be focused by special optical elements, since X-rays cannot be focused or redirected by conventional lenses and mirrors. The laser would damage targets by impulse kill (ablative shock). A thin 1-meter-long XRL operating at a wavelength of 20 nanometers supposedly would produce a beam with a divergence angle of 100 microradians. This angle is large compared to those achievable by lasers with longer wavelengths.

The United States is studying X-ray lasers of different wavelengths because a tenfold change in wavelength could alter the penetrating capability (brightness) a thousandfold. (In an underground nuclear test in 1980, an X-ray laser beam with a wavelength of 1.4 nanometers was supposedly attained; in another test in 1984 at the Lawrence Livermore National Laboratory, a wavelength of 15.5 nanometers was reached.) A wavelength of 0.1 nanometers (1 angstrom) may be the goal of SDI researchers. The United States also has not revealed the projected capabilities of the X-ray laser being considered, but studies have determined that a 1-megaton, bomb-pumped X-ray laser could deposit 100 million megajoules into a cone no narrower than 20 microradians. Since the pumping mechanism for any projected X-ray laser is at present disorganized and wasteful (like the pumping mechanism for excimer lasers), only a small percentage of the bomb's energy would end up in the laser beam, but even this could be a lethal weapon at several thousand kilometers. Still, an X-ray laser of great brightness and concentration would be required for boost-phase intercept. In a pop-up, submarine-launched mode of deployment near the Soviet Union, an X-ray laser of increased brightness and small wavelength might even be effective against fast-burn boosters by making use of the phenomenon of bleaching. *See* bleaching; pop-up technique.

yield: The energy released during a nuclear explosion; expressed in kilotons or megatons.

Yonas, Gerold: Chief scientist in the SDIO (1984–86). Yonas resigned from the organization to become vice president of electro-optic and high-energy systems at the Titan Corporation, La Jolla, California. When he worked at Sandia National Laboratories, he served on the Defensive Technological Studies team as chairman of the DEW panel.

Treaty Between the United States of America and the Union of Soviet Socialist Republics on the Limitation of Anti-Ballistic Missile Systems

Signed at Moscow May 26, 1972
Ratification advised by U.S. Senate August 3, 1972
Ratified by U.S. President September 30, 1972
Proclaimed by U.S. President October 3, 1972
Instruments of ratification exchanged October 3, 1972
Entered into force October 3, 1972

The United States of America and the Union of Soviet Socialist Republics, hereinafter referred to as the Parties,

Proceeding from the premise that nuclear war would have devastating consequences for all mankind,

Considering that effective measures to limit anti-ballistic missile systems would be a substantial factor in curbing the race in strategic offensive arms and would lead to a decrease in the risk of outbreak of war involving nuclear weapons,

Proceeding from the premise that the limitation of anti-ballistic missile systems, as well as certain agreed measures with respect to the limitation of strategic offensive arms, would contribute to the creation of more favorable conditions for further negotiations on limiting strategic arms,

Mindful of their obligations under Article VI of the Treaty on the Non-Proliferation of Nuclear Weapons,

Declaring their intention to achieve at the earliest possible date the cessation of the nuclear arms race and to take effective measures toward reductions in strategic arms, nuclear disarmament, and general and complete disarmament,

Desiring to contribute to the relaxation of international tension and the strengthening of trust between States,

Have agreed as follows:

Article I

1. Each Party undertakes to limit anti-ballistic missile (ABM) systems and to adopt other measures in accordance with the provisions of this Treaty.

2. Each Party undertakes not to deploy ABM systems for a defense of the territory of its country and not to provide a base for such a defense, and not to deploy ABM systems for defense of an individual region except as provided for in Article III of this Treaty.

Article II

1. For the purpose of this Treaty an ABM system is a system to counter strategic ballistic missiles or their elements in flight trajectory, currently consisting of:

   (a) ABM interceptor missiles, which are interceptor missiles constructed and deployed for an ABM role, or of a type tested in an ABM mode;

   (b) ABM launchers, which are launchers constructed and deployed for launching ABM interceptor missiles; and

   (c) ABM radars, which are radars constructed and deployed for an ABM role, or of a type tested in an ABM mode.

2. The ABM system components listed in paragraph 1 of this Article include those which are:
   (a) operational;
   (b) under construction;
   (c) undergoing testing;
   (d) undergoing overhaul, repair or conversion; or
   (e) mothballed.

Article III

Each Party undertakes not to deploy ABM systems or their components except that:

(a) within one ABM system deployment area having a radius of one hundred and fifty kilometers and centered on the Party's national capital, a Party may deploy: (1) no more than one hundred ABM launchers and no more than one hundred ABM interceptor missiles at launch sites, and (2) ABM radars within no more than six ABM radar complexes, the area of each complex being circular and having a diameter of no more than three kilometers; and

(b) within one ABM system deployment area having a radius of one hundred and fifty kilometers and containing ICBM silo launchers, a Party may deploy: (1) no more than one hundred ABM launchers and no more than one hundred ABM interceptor missiles at launch sites, (2) two large phased-array ABM radars comparable in potential to corresponding ABM radars operational or under construction on the date of signature of the Treaty in an ABM system deployment area containing ICBM silo launchers, and (3) no more than eighteen ABM radars each having a potential less than the potential of the smaller of the above-mentioned two large phased-array ABM radars.

Article IV

The limitations provided for in Article III shall not apply to ABM systems or their components used for development or testing, and located within current or additionally agreed test ranges. Each Party may have no more than a total of fifteen ABM launchers at test ranges.

Article V

1. Each Party undertakes not to develop, test, or deploy ABM systems or components which are sea-based, air-based, space-based or mobile land-based.

2. Each Party undertakes not to develop, test, or deploy ABM launchers for launching more than one ABM interceptor missile at a time from each launcher, not to modify deployed launchers to provide them with such a capability, not to develop, test, or deploy automatic or semi-automatic or other similar systems for rapid reload of ABM launchers.

Article VI

To enhance assurance of the effectiveness of the limitations on ABM systems and their components provided by the Treaty, each Party undertakes:

(a) not to give missiles, launchers, or radars, other than ABM interceptor missiles, ABM launchers, or ABM radars, capabilities to counter strategic ballistic missiles or their elements in flight trajectory, and not to test them in an ABM mode; and

(b) not to deploy in the future radars for early warning of strategic ballistic missile attack except at locations along the periphery of its national territory and oriented outward.

Article VII

Subject to the provisions of this Treaty, modernization and replacement of ABM systems or their components may be carried out.

Article VIII

ABM systems or their components in excess of the numbers or outside the areas specified in this Treaty, as well as ABM systems or their components prohibited by this Treaty, shall be destroyed or dismantled under agreed procedures within the shortest possible agreed period of time.

Article IX

To assure the viability and effectiveness of this Treaty, each Party undertakes not to transfer to other States, and not to deploy outside its national territory, ABM systems or their components limited by this Treaty.

Article X

Each Party undertakes not to assume any international obligations which would conflict with this Treaty.

Article XI

The Parties undertake to continue active negotiations for limitations on strategic offensive arms.

Article XII

1. For the purpose of providing assurance of compliance with the provisions of this Treaty, each Party shall use national technical means of verification at its disposal in a manner consistent with generally recognized principles of international law.

2. Each Party undertakes not to interfere with the national technical means of verification of the other Party operating in accordance with paragraph 1 of this Article.

3. Each Party undertakes not to use deliberate concealment measures which impede verification by national technical means of compliance with the provisions of this Treaty. This obligation shall not require changes in current construction, assembly, conversion, or overhaul practices.

Article XIII

1. To promote the objectives and implementation of the provisions of this Treaty, the Parties shall establish promptly a Standing Consultative Commission, within the framework of which they will:

(a) consider questions concerning compliance with the obligations assumed and related situations which may be considered ambiguous;

(b) provide on a voluntary basis such information as either Party considers necessary to assure confidence in compliance with the obligations assumed;

(c) consider questions involving unintended interference with national technical means of verification;

(d) consider possible changes in the strategic situation which have a bearing on the provisions of this Treaty;

(e) agree upon procedures and dates for destruction or dismantling of ABM systems or their components in cases provided for by the provisions of this Treaty;

(f) consider, as appropriate, possible proposals for further increasing the viability of this Treaty, including proposals for amendments in accordance with the provisions of this Treaty;

(g) consider, as appropriate, proposals for further measures aimed at limiting strategic arms.

2. The Parties through consultation shall establish, and may amend as appropriate, Regulations for the Standing Consultative Commission governing procedures, composition and other relevant matters.

Article XIV

1. Each Party may propose amendments to this Treaty. Agreed amendments shall enter into force in accordance with the procedures governing the entry into force of this Treaty.

2. Five years after entry into force of this Treaty, and at five-year intervals thereafter, the Parties shall together conduct a review of this Treaty.

Article XV

1. This Treaty shall be of unlimited duration.

2. Each Party shall, in exercising its national sovereignty, have the right to withdraw from this Treaty if it decides that extraordinary events related to the subject matter of this Treaty have jeopardized its supreme

interests. It shall give notice of its decision to the other Party six months prior to withdrawal from the Treaty. Such notice shall include a statement of the extraordinary events the notifying Party regards as having jeopardized its supreme interests.

Article XVI

1. This Treaty shall be subject to ratification in accordance with the constitutional procedures of each Party. The Treaty shall enter into force on the day of the exchange of instruments of ratification.

2. This Treaty shall be registered pursuant to Article 102 of the Charter of the United Nations.

DONE at Moscow on May 26, 1972, in two copies, each in the English and Russian languages, both texts being equally authentic.

FOR THE UNITED STATES OF AMERICA	**FOR THE UNION OF SOVIET SOCIALIST REPUBLICS**
|s| RICHARD NIXON	|s| L. I. BREZHNEV
President of the United States of America	*General Secretary of the Central Committee of the CPSU*

Agreed Statements, Common Understandings, and Unilateral Statements Regarding the Treaty Between the United States of America and the Union of Soviet Socialist Republics on the Limitation of Anti-Ballistic Missiles

1. Agreed Statements

The document set forth below was agreed upon and initiated by the Heads of the Delegations on May 26, 1972 (letter designations added);

AGREED STATEMENTS REGARDING THE TREATY BETWEEN THE UNITED STATES OF AMERICA AND THE UNION OF SOVIET SOCIALIST REPUBLICS ON THE LIMITATION OF ANTI-BALLISTIC MISSILE SYSTEMS

[A]

The Parties understand that, in addition to the ABM radars which may be deployed in accordance with subparagraph (a) of Article III of the Treaty, those non-phased-array ABM radars operational on the date of signature of the Treaty within the ABM system deployment area for defense of the national capital may be retained.

[B]

The Parties understand that the potential (the product of mean emitted power in watts and antenna area in square meters) of the smaller of the two large phased-array ABM radars referred to in subparagraph (b) of Article III of the Treaty is considered for purposes of the Treaty to be three million.

167

[C]

The Parties understand that the center of the ABM system deployment area centered on the national capital and the center of the ABM system deployment area containing ICBM silo launchers for each Party shall be separated by no less than thirteen hundred kilometers.

[D]

In order to insure fulfillment of the obligation not to deploy ABM systems and their components except as provided in Article III of the Treaty, the Parties agree that in the event ABM systems based on other physical principles and including components capable of substituting for ABM interceptor missiles, ABM launchers, or ABM radars are created in the future, specific limitations on such systems and their components would be subject to discussion in accordance with Article XIII and agreement in accordance with Article XIV of the Treaty.

[E]

The Parties understand that Article V of the Treaty includes obligations not to develop, test, or deploy ABM interceptor missiles for the delivery by each ABM interceptor missile of more than one independently guided warhead.

[F]

The Parties agree not to deploy phased-array radars having a potential (the product of mean emitted power in watts and antenna area in square meters) exceeding three million, except as provided for in Articles III, IV, and VI of the Treaty, or except for the purposes of tracking objects in outer space or for use as national technical means of verification.

[G]

The Parties understand that Article IX of the Treaty includes the obligation of the US and the USSR not to provide to other States technical descriptions or blue prints specially worked out for the construction of ABM systems and their components limited by the Treaty.

2. Common Understandings

Common understanding of the Parties on the following matters was reached during the negotiations:

A. Location of ICBM Defenses

The U.S. Delegation made the following statement on May 26, 1972:

Article III of the ABM Treaty provides for each side one ABM system deployment area centered on its national capital and one ABM system deployment area containing ICBM silo launchers. The two sides have registered agreement on the following statement: "The Parties understand that the center of the ABM system deployment area centered on the national capital and the center of the ABM system deployment area containing ICBM silo launchers for each Party shall be separated by no less than thirteen hundred kilometers." In this connection, the U.S. side notes that its ABM system deployment area for defense of ICBM silo launchers, located west of the Mississippi River, will be centered in the Grand Forks ICBM silo launcher deployment area. (See Agreed Statement [C].)

B. ABM Test Ranges

The U.S. Delegation made the following statement on April 26, 1972:

Article IV of the ABM Treaty provides that "the limitations provided for in Article III shall not apply to ABM systems or their components used for development or testing, and located within current or additionally agreed test ranges." We believe it would be useful to assure that there is no misunderstanding as to current ABM test ranges. It is our understanding that ABM test ranges encompass the area within which ABM components are located for test purposes. The current U.S. ABM test ranges are at White Sands, New Mexico, and at Kwajalein Atoll, and the current Soviet ABM test range is near Sary Shagan in Kazakhstan. We consider that non-phased array radars of types used for range safety or instrumentation purposes may be located outside of ABM test ranges. We interpret the reference in Article IV to "additionally agreed test ranges" to mean that ABM components will not be located at any other test ranges without prior agreement between our Governments that there will be such additional ABM test ranges.

On May 5, 1972, the Soviet Delegation stated that there was a common understanding on what ABM test ranges were, that the use of the types of non-ABM radars for range safety or instrumentation was not limited under the Treaty, that the reference in Article IV to "additionally agreed" test ranges was sufficiently clear, and that national means permitted identifying current test ranges.

C. Mobile ABM Systems

On January 29, 1972, the U.S. Delegation made the following statement:

Article V(1) of the Joint Draft Text of the ABM Treaty includes an undertaking not to develop, test, or deploy mobile land-based ABM systems and their components. On May 5, 1971, the U.S. side indicated that, in its view, a prohibition on deployment of mobile ABM systems and components would rule out the deployment of ABM launchers and radars which were not permanent fixed types. At that time, we asked for the Soviet view of this interpretation. Does the Soviet side agree with the U.S. side's interpretation put forward on May 5, 1971?

On April 13, 1972, the Soviet Delegation said there is a general common understanding on this matter.

D. Standing Consultative Commission

Ambassador Smith made the following statement on May 22, 1972:

The United States proposes that the sides agree that, with regard to initial implementation of the ABM Treaty's Article XIII on the Standing Consultative Commission (SCC) and of the consultation Articles to the Interim Agreement on offensive arms and the Accidents Agreement,[1] agreement establishing the SCC will be worked out early in the follow-on SALT negotiations; until that is completed, the following arrangements will prevail: when SALT is in session, any consultation desired by either side under these Articles can be carried out by the two SALT Delegations; when SALT is not in session, *ad hoc* arrangements for any desired consultations under these Articles may be made through diplomatic channels.

Minister Semenov replied that, on an *ad referendum* basis, he could agree that the U.S. statement corresponded to the Soviet understanding.

E. Standstill

On May 6, 1972, Minister Semenov made the following statement:

In an effort to accommodate the wishes of the U.S. side, the Soviet Delegation is prepared to proceed on the basis that the two sides will

---

[1] See Article 7 of Agreement to Reduce the Risk of Outbreak of Nuclear War Between the United States of America and the Union of Soviet Socialist Republics, signed Sept. 30, 1971.

in fact observe the obligations of both the Interim Agreement and the ABM Treaty beginning from the date of signature of these two documents.

In reply, the U.S. Delegation made the following statement on May 20, 1972:

The U.S. agrees in principle with the Soviet statement made on May 6 concerning observance of obligations beginning from date of signature but we would like to make clear our understanding that this means that, pending ratification and acceptance, neither side would take any action prohibited by the agreements after they had entered into force. This understanding would continue to apply in the absence of notification by either signatory of its intention not to proceed with ratification or approval.

The Soviet Delegation indicated agreement with the U.S. statement.

3. Unilateral Statements

The following noteworthy unilateral statements were made during the negotiations by the United States Delegation:

A. Withdrawal from the ABM Treaty

On May 9, 1972, Ambassador Smith made the following statement:

The U.S. Delegation has stressed the importance the U.S. Government attaches to achieving agreement on more complete limitations on strategic offensive arms, following agreement on an ABM Treaty and on an Interim Agreement on certain measures with respect to the limitation of strategic offensive arms. The U.S. Delegation believes that an objective of the follow-on negotiations should be to constrain and reduce on a long-term basis threats to the survivability of our respective strategic retaliatory forces. The USSR Delegation has also indicated that the objectives of SALT would remain unfulfilled without the achievement of an agreement providing for more complete limitations on strategic offensive arms. Both sides recognize that the initial agreements would be steps toward the achievement of more complete limitations on strategic arms. If an agreement providing for more complete strategic offensive arms limitations were not achieved within five years, U.S. supreme interests could be jeopardized. Should that occur, it would constitute a basis for withdrawal from the ABM Treaty. The

U.S. does not wish to see such a situation occur, nor do we believe that the USSR does. It is because we wish to prevent such a situation that we emphasize the importance the U.S. Government attaches to achievement of more complete limitations on strategic offensive arms. The U.S. Executive will inform the Congress, in connection with Congressional consideration of the ABM Treaty and the Interim Agreement, of this statement of the U.S. position.

B. Tested in ABM Mode

On April 7, 1972, the U.S. Delegation made the following statement:

Article II of the Joint Text Draft uses the term "tested in an ABM mode," in defining ABM components, and Article VI includes certain obligations concerning such testing. We believe that the sides should have a common understanding of this phrase. First, we would note that the testing provisions of the ABM Treaty are intended to apply to testing which occurs after the date of signature of the Treaty, and not to any testing which may have occurred in the past. Next, we would amplify the remarks we have made on this subject during the previous Helsinki phase by setting forth the objectives which govern the U.S. view on the subject, namely, while prohibiting testing of non-ABM components for ABM purposes; not to prevent testing of ABM components, and not to prevent testing of non-ABM components for non-ABM purposes. To clarify our interpretation of "tested in an ABM mode," we note that we would consider a launcher, missile or radar to be "tested in an ABM mode" if, for example, any of the following events occur: (1) a launcher is used to launch an ABM interceptor missile, (2) an interceptor missile is flight tested against a target vehicle which has a flight trajectory with characteristics of a strategic ballistic missile flight trajectory, or is flight tested in conjunction with the test of an ABM interceptor missile or an ABM radar at the same test range, or is flight tested to an altitude inconsistent with interception of targets against which air defenses are deployed, (3) a radar makes measurements on a cooperative target vehicle of the kind referred to in item (2) above during the reentry portion of its trajectory or makes measurements in conjunction with the test of an ABM interceptor missile or an ABM radar at the same test range. Radars used for purposes such as range safety or instrumentation would be exempt from application of these criteria.

C. No-Transfer Article of ABM Treaty

On April 18, 1972, the U.S. Delegation made the following statement:

In regard to this Article [IX], I have a brief and I believe self-explanatory statement to make. The U.S. side wishes to make clear that the provisions of this Article do not set a precedent for whatever provision may be considered for a Treaty on Limiting Strategic Offensive Arms. The question of transfer of strategic offensive arms is a far more complex issue, which may require a different solution.

D. No Increase in Defense of Early Warning Radars

On July 28, 1970, the U.S. Delegation made the following statement:

Since Hen House radars [Soviet ballistic missile early warning radars] can detect and track ballistic missile warheads at great distances, they have a significant ABM potential. Accordingly, the U.S. would regard any increase in the defenses of such radars by surface-to-air missiles as inconsistent with an agreement.

The Conclusion of President Reagan's March 23, 1983, Speech on Defense Spending and Defensive Technology

Now, thus far tonight I've shared with you my thoughts on the problems of national security we must face together. My predecessors in the Oval Office have appeared before you on other occasions to describe the threat posed by Soviet power and have proposed steps to address that threat. But, since the advent of nuclear weapons, those steps have been increasingly directed toward deterrence of aggression through the promise of retaliation.

This approach to stability through offensive threat has worked. We and our allies have succeeded in preventing nuclear war for more than three decades. In recent months, however, my advisers, including in particular the Joint Chiefs of Staff, have underscored the necessity to break out of a future that relies solely on offensive retaliation for our security.

Over the course of these discussions, I've become more and more deeply convinced that the human spirit must be capable of rising above dealing with other nations and human beings by threatening their existence. Feeling this way, I believe we must thoroughly examine every opportunity for reducing tensions and for introducing greater stability into the strategic calculus on both sides.

One of the most important contributions we can make is, of course, to lower the level of all arms, and particularly nuclear arms. We're engaged right now in several negotiations with the Soviet Union to bring about a mutual reduction of weapons. I will report to you a week from tomorrow my thoughts on that score. But let me just say, I'm totally committed to this course.

If the Soviet Union will join with us in our effort to achieve major arms reduction, we will have succeeded in stabilizing the nuclear balance. Nevertheless, it will still be necessary to rely on the specter of retaliation, on mutual threat. And that's a sad commentary on the human condition. Wouldn't it be better to save lives than to avenge them? Are we not capable of demonstrating our peaceful intentions by applying all our abilities and our ingenuity to achieving a truly lasting stability? I think we are. Indeed, we must.

After careful consideration with my advisers, including the Joint Chiefs of Staff, I believe there is a way. Let me share with you a vision of the future which offers hope. It is that we embark on a program to counter the awesome Soviet missile threat with measures that are defensive. Let us turn to the very strengths in technology that spawned our great industrial base and that have given us the quality of life we enjoy today.

What if free people could live secure in the knowledge that their security did not rest upon the threat of instant U.S. retaliation to deter a Soviet attack, that we could intercept and destroy strategic ballistic missiles before they reached our own soil or that of our allies?

I know this is a formidable, technical task, one that may not be accomplished before the end of this century. Yet, current technology has attained a level of sophistication where it's reasonable for us to begin this effort. It will take years, probably decades of effort on many fronts. There will be failures and setbacks, just as there will be successes and breakthroughs. And as we proceed, we must remain constant in preserving the nuclear deterrent and maintaining a solid capability for flexible response. But isn't it worth every investment necessary to free the world from the threat of nuclear war? We know it is.

In the meantime, we will continue to pursue real reductions in nuclear arms, negotiating from a position of strength that can be ensured only by modernizing our strategic forces. At the same time, we must take steps to reduce the risk of a conventional military conflict escalating to nuclear war by improving our nonnuclear capabilities.

America does possess—now—the technologies to attain very significant improvements in the effectiveness of our conventional, nonnuclear forces. Proceeding boldly with these new technologies, we can significantly reduce any incentive that the Soviet Union may have to threaten attack against the United States or its allies.

As we pursue our goal of defensive technologies, we recognize that our allies rely upon our strategic offensive power to deter attacks against them. Their vital interests and ours are inextricably linked. Their safety and ours are one. And no change in technology can or will alter that reality. We must and shall continue to honor our commitments.

I clearly recognize that defensive systems have limitations and raise certain problems and ambiguities. If paired with offensive systems, they can be viewed as fostering an aggressive policy, and no one wants that. But, with these considerations firmly in mind, I call upon the scientific communities in our country, those who gave us nuclear weapons, to turn their great talents now to the cause of mankind and world peace, to give us the means of rendering these nuclear weapons impotent and obsolete.

Tonight, consistent with our obligations of the ABM Treaty and recognizing the need for closer consultation with our allies, I'm taking an important first step. I am directing a comprehensive and intensive effort to define a long-term research and development program to begin to achieve our ultimate goal of eliminating the threat posed by strategic nuclear missiles. This could pave the way for arms control measures to eliminate the weapons themselves. We seek neither military superiority nor political advantage. Our only purpose—one all people share—is to search for ways to reduce the danger of nuclear war.

My fellow Americans, tonight we're launching an effort which holds the promise of changing the course of human history. There will be risks, and results take time. But I believe we can do it. As we cross this threshold, I ask for your prayers and your support.

Thank you, good night, and God bless you.

Defensive Technologies Study Team

Study Team Leadership

Dr. James C. Fletcher
  Study Chairman — University of Pittsburgh

Dr. Harold M. Agnew
  Vice Chairman — General Atomic Technologies Inc.

Major General John C. Toomay
  Deputy Chairman — U.S. Air Force (Ret.)

Dr. Alexander H. Flax
  Deputy Chairman — Institute for Defense Analysis

Mr. John L. Gardner
  Executive Secretary — Office of the Secretary of Defense

Major Simon P. Worden
  Executive Military Assistant — Office of the Secretary of Defense

Conventional Weapons Panel

Dr. Julian Davidson
  Panel Chairman — Science Applications Inc.

Dr. Delmar Bergen — Los Alamos National Laboratory

Mr. T. Jeff Coleman — Coleman Research Inc.

Dr. Clarke DeJonge — Science Applications Inc.

Dr. Harry D. Fair — Defense Advanced Research Projects Agency

Dr. James Katechis — U.S. Army Ballistic Missile Defense Systems Command

Dr. Joseph R. Mayersak — USAF Armament Division

Lt. Col. Miles Clements
  Military Assistant — Headquarters, Department of the Army

Lt. Col. Peter E. Gleszer
  Military Assistant — Headquarters, Department of the Army

Systems Concepts Panel

Dr. Edward T. Gerry
  Panel Chairman (Boost-Phase
    Systems)
	W. J. Schafer Associates Inc.

Dr. Wayne R. Winton
  Panel Chairman (Midcourse
    Systems)
	Sparta Inc.

Mr. Charles R. Wieser
  Panel Chairman (Terminal-
    Phase Systems)
	Physical Dynamics Inc.

Dr. J. E. Lowder	Sparta Inc.
Dr. James R. Fisher	U.S. Army Ballistic Missile Defense Systems Command
Dr. Louis C. Marquet	Defense Advanced Research Projects Agency

Directed-Energy Weapons Panel

Dr. Gerold Yonas Panel Chairman	Sandia National Laboratories
Dr. J. Richard Airey	Science Applications Inc.
Dr. Robert T. Andrews	Lawrence Livermore National Laboratory
Dr. Richard J. Briggs	Lawrence Livermore National Laboratory
Dr. Gregory H. Canavan	Los Alamos National Laboratory
Dr. Robert W. Selden	Los Alamos National Laboratory
Dr. Petras Avizonis	USAF Weapons Laboratory
Captain Richard J. Joseph	Defense Nuclear Agency
Dr. Joseph A. Mangano	Defense Advanced Research Projects Agency
Dr. Robert C. Sepucha	Defense Advanced Research Projects Agency
Captain Alan Evans Military Assistant	USAF Systems Command

Systems Integration Panel

Lieutenant General
  Kenneth B. Cooper
  Panel Chairman
	U.S. Army (Ret.)
	Systems Planning Corporation

Mr. Wallace D. Henderson	Braddock, Dunn and McDonald
Mr. Robert T. Poppe	General Research Corporation
Mr. John M. Bachkosky	Office of the Secretary of Defense

Surveillance, Acquisition, Tracking, and Kill Assessment Panel

Dr. John L. Allen Panel Chairman	John Allen Associates Inc.
Dr. George F. Aroyan	Hughes Aircraft Company
Dr. John A. Jamieson	John Jamieson Inc.
Mr. William Z. Lemnios	Massachusetts Institute of Technology
Mr. Dennis P. Murray	Research and Development Associates
Mr. Robert G. Richards	Aerojet Electronics Systems
Mr. Fritz Steudel	Raytheon Corporation
Lt. (jg) Patricia A. O'Rourke Military Assistant	Office of the Chief of Naval Operations

Countermeasures and Tactics Panel

Dr. Alexander H. Flax Panel Chairman	Institute for Defense Analysis
Dr. Robert B. Barker	Lawrence Livermore National Laboratory
Dr. Robert G. Clem	Sandia National Laboratories
Dr. Walter R. Sooy	Lawrence Livermore National Laboratory
Dr. James W. Somers	Defense Nuclear Agency

Battle Management, C3, and Data Processing Panel

Dr. Brockway McMillan Panel Chairman	Private Consultant
Dr. Duane A. Adams	Private Consultant
Dr. Harry I. Davis	Private Consultant
Mr. J. R. Logie	Private Consultant
Dr. Robert E. Nicholls	Massachusetts Institute of Technology/Lincoln Laboratory
Mr. Robert Yost	Science Applications Inc.

Executive Scientific Review Group

Dr. Edward Frieman Group Chairman	Science Applications Inc.
Lt. Col. Michael Havey	Office of Science and Technology Policy
Dr. Solomon J. Buchsbaum	Bell Laboratories
Mr. Daniel Fink	Private Consultant
Mr. Bert Fowler	Mitre Corporation
Dr. Eugene Fubini	Private Consultant
Admiral Bobby R. Inman	U.S. Navy (Ret.) Microelectronics and Computer Technology Corporation
Dr. Michael May	Lawrence Livermore National Laboratory
General E. C. Meyer	U.S. Army (Ret.)
Professor William A. Nierenberg	Scripps Institute of Oceanography
Dr. David Packard	Hewlett-Packard Company